FRIENDS
OF ACP

"*Predators and Child Mol...* ...cts noted sex crimes professional Robin Sax's tirele... ...r-ents in understanding and coping with the per... ...d sexual abuse. With a keen eye toward prevention ...... along the dark path of sex crimes against children from perpetration to prosecution. Along the way she offers families help for healing and recovery. Packed with carefully constructed questions and compelling answers about sexual abuse, this is a must-read for all parents, as well as every other person who has responsibility for the care and safety of children."

Larry A. Morris, PhD
Clinical and forensic psychologist, coauthor of
Males at Risk: The Other Side of Child Sexual Abuse,
and author of *Dangerous Women: Why Mothers, Daughters, and Sisters
Become Stalkers, Molesters, and Murderers*

"Insightful and practical . . . Robin Sax has written a book that's easy to understand and easy to apply to real life. It's obvious that Sax knows firsthand the dangers that our families are up against. It's a must read for any parent who wants to take control over the safety of his/her child."

Rabbi Jonathan Aaron
Associate rabbi and director of Education at Temple Emanuel

"*Predators and Child Molesters* is an outstanding practical guide to safety. Owning and reading this book is like having a guardian angel give directions, guiding parents from the state of being controlled to the state of being in control. Sex crimes prosecutor and parent Robin Sax speaks from experience. Her voice is loud and clear. Listen up!"

Susan Murphy Milano
Violence expert and author of *Defending Our Lives*
and *Moving Out Moving On*

"Robin Sax is the expert in answering all of the most asked questions in *Predators and Child Molesters*. These are the questions parents are afraid to ask but think about frequently. It couples her knowledge as a district attorney specializing in sex crimes with her own parenting skills and delivers a powerful wealth of information. As a former sex crimes detective and parent, I found myself engrossed within the book's pages and was truly in awe of her intelligence into the frightening subject of child molesters. . . . It should become a requirement for parents everywhere to read."

Stacy Dittrich
Former detective, law enforcement media consultant,
and author of *Murder behind the Badge: True Stories of Cops Who Kill*

"Robin Sax has used her extensive experience as a deputy district attorney, specializing in assaults on children, to write the definitive book about keeping children safe. With a no-nonsense tone, Sax teaches parents what they need to do to protect their children of all ages. This is a most valuable resource for any parent!"

Dr. Jenn Berman
Author of *The A to Z Guide to Raising Happy Confident Kids*

"Predators aren't only found in the jungles or on the savannah; they are just down the street, at the mall, and, sometimes, in our very own homes. But unlike the lions and tigers of the wild, domestic human hunters can go unrecognized until it is too late. In this must-read book, Robin Sax shares her expertise from years as a sex crimes prosecutor, helping parents understand how pedophiles operate and what they can do to make sure their children don't fall victim to them."

Pat Brown
Criminal profiler

"*Predators and Child Molesters* answers everything you wanted to ask and tells everything you need to know to prevent your worst nightmare and possible lifelong torment for your child. Sax writes in an easy-to-read format, providing practical answers for keeping youngsters safe. This is a must read for every parent or anyone who cares for kids."

Mark Goulston
Huffington Post

"If you're a new prosecutor, rookie police officer, or parent, here is your Bible for defense against child predators. We want to tell our children monsters aren't real, but they are. They walk among us everyday in disguise. Thanks to Robin Sax we know how to fight them—and win!"

Sheryl McCollum, MS
Director of Cold Case Investigative Research Institute

PREDATORS *and* CHILD MOLESTERS

PREDATORS *and*
CHILD MOLESTERS

What Every Parent Needs to Know to Keep Kids Safe

*A Sex Crimes DA Answers 100 of the
Most Asked Questions*

ROBIN SAX

Prometheus Books
59 John Glenn Drive
Amherst, New York 14228-2119

Published 2009 by Prometheus Books

Inquiries should be addressed to
Prometheus Books
59 John Glenn Drive
Amherst, New York 14228–2119
VOICE: 716–691–0133, ext. 210
FAX: 716–691–0137
WWW.PROMETHEUSBOOKS.COM

13 12 11 10 09   5 4 3 2

Library of Congress Cataloging-in-Publication Data

Sax, Robin.
    Predators and child molesters : what every parent needs to know to keep kids safe :
a sex crimes DA answers 100 of the most asked questions / by Robin Sax.
        p. cm.
    ISBN 978–1–59102–712–6 (pbk. : alk. paper)
    1. Child sexual abuse—United States. 2. Child sexual abuse—United States—Prevention.
3. Child abuse—United States. I. Title.

HV6570.2.S39 2009
362.760973—dc22

                                                                    2008054572

Printed in the United States on acid-free paper

To my children—
Hannah, Jason, and Jeremy,
forever and always.

CONTENTS

Acknowledgments   13

Foreword   17

Introduction   19

Author's Note   21

PART ONE: RECOGNIZING THE PREDATORS:
MOLESTERS, PEDOPHILES, AND
OPPORTUNISTS

1. How prevalent is child sexual abuse?   23
2. How do you define child sexual abuse?   ·   25
3. What are the differences between a pedophile,
   an opportunist, a molester, and a predator?   27
4. What acts are considered sexually abusive?   31
5. If the child consents, is it still considered sexual abuse?   33
6. How prevalent is sexual abuse of males?   34
7. Are "Peeping Toms" and people who expose themselves
   considered sex offenders?   35
8. What is Megan's Law?   37
9. What does a molester look like?   39
10. What is "grooming"?   40
11. Where do molesters seek their victims?   42
12. Why are children susceptible to sexual abuse?   43
13. Where do molesters live?   44
14. Why do people molest?   45

15. What is the relationship between
pornography and child molestation?   46

PART TWO: TALKING TO KIDS ABOUT RISKS AND
RECOGNIZING POTENTIAL PROBLEMS

16. How often should I talk to my children
about preventing sexual abuse?   49
17. How can I teach my kids about personal safety
without scaring them?   51
18. Is it OK to tell my children news stories about
sexually assaulted children?   54
19. Are Internet predators different from other predators?
Why are they so successful?   55
20. What should my family's rules be regarding our children's
use of the Internet?   58
21. Should I allow my child on social-networking sites like
MySpace, Facebook, or Second Life?   60
22. Should I hack into my kids' computers and monitor their
Web site usage?   61
23. What factors make someone more likely to
sexually abuse a child?   63
24. What should I do about sleepovers?   65
25. Can schools hire a teacher who has been accused of
sex acts with children?   67
26. Do schools do background checks on employees such as
teachers, staff, and administrators?   69
27. Should I let my child play outside in the neighborhood?   70
28. How can I find out if registered sex offenders live near me? 71
29. As a single mom, what should I do if I learn that
the man I'm dating is a sex offender?   73
30. As a divorced dad, is it OK if I bathe my preschool daughter? 74
31. How should I screen a babysitter or nanny?   75
32. Should I get a "nanny-cam" or other surveillance product?   80

PART THREE: RECOGNIZING ABUSE

33. Should I report a suspected child abuser to the police
or do I need tangible evidence? 83
34. What are the signs that a child has been improperly touched? 84
35. What are the potential warning signs of teacher misconduct? 85
36. What are the qualities of unnatural sexual behavior? 87
37. What do I do if I am uncomfortable with the way
someone acted, even though he never touched my child
or said anything directly sexual? 88
38. What should I do if my child discloses sexual assault? 89
39. What if I don't believe my child? 90
40. How late is too late to report sexual abuse? 91
41. Who are mandated reporters and what are their responsibilities? 93
42. What should I do if I suspect a child, other than mine,
is being touched? 94
43. What is the difference between a SCAR and a police report? 95
44. What makes kids disclose molestation? 97
45. What makes kids *not* disclose molestation? 98
46. How do I know if my child is telling the truth? 98
47. Can a man or boy still have an erection or ejaculate
if he is frightened? 100
48. How is sexual assault related to abduction? 101
49. What is an Amber Alert? 102

PART FOUR: REPORTING SEXUAL ABUSE

50. What kind of evidence is considered "corroboration"
of child sexual abuse? 103
51. What are the general stages of crime scene investigation
as it relates to child sexual assault? 105
52. What happens if there is a sexual assault disclosure
during a divorce case? 108
53. Can a polygraph be used to validate a child's disclosure
of sexual abuse? 109
54. What is "child sexual abuse accommodation syndrome"? 110

55. How do you find a predator whose identity
    my child doesn't know?   111
56. Under what circumstances will Child Protective Services (CPS)
    take my child away from me?   113
57. Whom should I call first if my child discloses sexual abuse?   114
58. What will the police do if I report the abuse?   115
59. Will an offending parent be deported if in this country illegally? 116
60. What if the victim is not a citizen?   117
61. What is a multidisciplinary team?   118
62. What is a forensic interview?   120
63. How many people will my child need to talk to?   122
64. Will the interview be videotaped?   123
65. Can I watch the interview?   124
66. Will my child need to have a medical or physical exam?
    Is it invasive or painful?   125

PART FIVE: GOING TO COURT

67. How do you determine whether a child can testify in court?   127
68. What is the difference between criminal court, civil court,
    family court, and dependency court?   130
69. What rights do victims have from governmental agencies?   131
70. What makes a case qualify to be filed?   133
71. What happens if a criminal case is *not* filed?   134
72. Who files a criminal case and what can be charged?   136
73. How long does a prosecutor have to file charges?   138
74. What if the victim or parent does not want to file charges?   139
75. Can a parent file a civil case?   139
76. Can my child's identity be shielded?   140
77. Are courtrooms closed in sexual assault cases?   141
78. What are the typical stages of the criminal court process?   142
79. How long does the criminal process take?   146
80. How do you prepare a child to testify in court?   146
81. What special procedures are in place for
    child sexual assault victims in court?   148
82. If a case is filed, will my child need to testify in court?   149

83. If my child has received a subpoena, what happens next?   150
84. Can't my child just write out a statement or testify
      via closed-circuit TV?   152
85. Can I watch my child testify?   152
86. What are the typical defenses in child sexual assault cases?   154
87. What is Jessica's Law?   156
88. Does the victim have a say in the perpetrator's sentencing?   157
89. What are the usual sentences/punishments for sex crimes?   159
90. Is registering as a sex offender a lifelong requirement?   160
91. Can child victims get a protective order or restraining order?   161
92. What happens if my child or someone else receives threats
      from the perpetrator?   162

PART SIX: HEALING AND MOVING ON

93. What kind of financial resources are available for the victim?   165
94. Can molesters be cured?   166
95. How should I talk to my child about the abuse?   167
96. What is the usual healing process for a victim of abuse?   168
97. Whose fault is it that my child was molested?   171
98. Can my child victim turn into an adult perpetrator?   172
99. Can I tell my abused daughter that she is still a virgin?   173
100. How long does the healing process take?   174

APPENDIX: WHERE CAN I GO FOR MORE INFORMATION?

175

ACKNOWLEDGMENTS

Every day I am amazed and thankful for the wonderful people who have helped me become the person I am today. You are my teachers, my colleagues, my friends, and my family, who have always supported me with my projects and ideas. You know who you are, and I thank each of you from the bottom of my heart.

First and foremost, I owe a humongous shout-out to my family. Though small, we are a tight and goofy group who make every day a new learning experience and another reason to be grateful and thankful.

To Andy, I thank my lucky stars for you every day. I appreciate your being my cheerleader, my co-parent, my husband, and my best friend. There is no one else in the world who could deal with me, and I know that. I love you. (Can you believe I am in the Library of Congress now?)

To Hannah, thank you for (almost) always being patient when I said, "One more minute." You have taught me both how to negotiate and how to listen. I love you from here to the moon and back again.

To Jason and Jeremy, I am so grateful that you didn't succeed in scaring me away like you did with all the "others." You two are the best stepsons. You were my first parenting teachers, and I wouldn't be the stepmom I am today without your love, challenges, and acceptance. I am grateful to have you in my life.

To Mom and Dad for always being there as my parents, protectors, and friends. You have been immensely supportive. I thank Dad for teaching me how to run around at a million miles an hour and Mom for reminding me to slow down. I promise I am close to taking your sound advice to get some sleep. I love you both.

To Heather and Scott, thank you for always being there with some good family dish to make me laugh and smile. Thank you for your love, kindness, and advice. And particularly to Scott for bringing me Brian Chang, my research assistant extraordinaire to whom I will forever be indebted!

To Aunt Vic and Uncle David, thank you for being reliable and always available for me to count on with words of encouragement and a darn good meal to help energize me and make me laugh.

To Mary and Royce, now do you understand why I haven't seen you in a year? I so appreciate your understanding and patience as I wrote this (and all) of my book(s).

To Bill and Dolly, thank you for reading, proofreading, and supporting me in this and all my projects and endeavors. And most importantly, thank you for always flying to us!

To Primo, the dog, for needing to pee every morning at 5 a.m., which forced me to get out of bed to write.

A sincere heartfelt thank you to Marc Klaas, who took the time out of his busy life of advocacy to write the foreword to my book. Your work on behalf of victims is not only admirable but also appreciated.

A special thanks to my friends at the DA's office who smiled when I told them I had a new project and who have always supported all my endeavors. I am starting with those with whom I have shared a nine-by-twelve space—Mary Hanlon Stone and Elena Camaras, both of whom know what it means to be a "sister."

To all my "bosses" for the hard work you do on behalf of the people of the State of California every day, specifically (in alphabetical order, not chain-of-command), Jane Blissert, Steve Cooley, Richard Doyle, Teresa Gomez, and John Lynch for being supportive in my endeavors and backing me through both wonderful and difficult times of career growth.

To my pals at Stuart House for all the learning, commiserating, and case analysis. Your work is tireless and always underappreciated. Well, I appreciate each of you: Lili Gonzalez, Brad McCart, Mara McIlvain, Jane Hallady, Susan Hardie, Doris Lemieux, Sophia Lund, Danielle Ramos, Mercedes Mendoza, Adrienne Dattrice, Melissa Melendez.

To the professionals whom I constantly call on for advice and who always come through with answers and support. Thank you, Sergeant Dan Scott, Detective Esther Reyes, Detective Vonnie Benjamin, Alma Burke, and Rape Treatment Center In-House Counsel Beth Cranston.

Then there are my friends, the yatches, the soul sisters, the girls who have made me appreciate the bond of friendship and sisterhood. I never thought that my world would be made of amazing women. I am so lucky to have you guys. I am listing you alphabetically so no one gets bent out of shape. I love each of you in your own very special way—Beth Golden Christopher, Kathryn Cavanaugh, Stephanie Cornick, Stacy Dittrich, Mandi Dyner, Dana Guerin, Kiko Korne, Susan Murphy Milano, Tamara Miller, Eva Stodel, Jillian Straus, and Ellie Zexter. Who would have ever guessed that women could be so cool?

And what would I do without Dr. Mark Goulston? I would be remiss if I didn't recognize Dr. Mark as the amazing mentor and friend who has helped keep me sane both professionally and personally.

To Dana Pretzer for always giving me a place to be heard and speak my mind. I am grateful to you and all of the work you do on behalf of victims each and every day.

A special thank you to Prometheus Books but particularly Steven L. Mitchell and Heather Ammermuller for your tireless efforts and energy in making this book a reality and more importantly for also editing through my garbly gook to make sense of my words, commas and all.

Thank you to Claire Gerus, who belongs in every category above— practically family, certainly a soul sister, a colleague, a friend, a confidant, an editor, a professional, and the world's best literary agent in the whole wide world. Your love, energy, commitment, and belief in me means the world.

Last and certainly never least, I appreciate all of the victims, survivors, and family members who have dealt with sexual abuse and who have allowed me into their lives to help. I have learned so much from you. You have taught me how to be strong, brave, and steadfast. You all inspire me each and every day.

To my two other Marks—Kaplan and Geragos—I thank you for your support and wisdom both as friends and as colleagues.

FOREWORD

Marc Klaas

When my daughter Polly was kidnapped, raped, and murdered in 1993, very little was known about the sexual abuse and exploitation of children. Neither the federal nor the state governments were tracking these crimes; therefore, the prevalence of sex crimes against children was unknown. There was no mandate to register sex offenders, let alone notify the community of their existence. Sex offenders, particularly those who offended against children, existed under the radar, committing crime with impunity, secure in the knowledge that their victims, alone and afraid, would not reveal their shame.

In 1993 sex crimes against children were America's dirty little secret, but today much has changed. With heightened awareness, all facets of society are much better educated to the risks faced by all our children. Parents are more willing to sit around the kitchen table and discuss safety issues with their children. Law enforcement has adopted a multidisciplinary approach to investigating these crimes that minimizes trauma to the victim and better preserves evidence. Media, particularly the cable news outlets, oftentimes lead their newscasts with the latest high-profile crime involving a child. Finally, policy makers have responded to sex crimes against children by passing laws that sentence perpetrators to much harsher prison terms, force them to register prior to being released into society, and notify the community whenever a registered sex offender moves into a neighborhood.

However, this sea change in knowledge and information is understandably accompanied by confusion, myth, and misinformation. Fortunately, *Predators and Child Molesters: What Every Parent Needs to Know to Keep Kids Safe*, by Los Angeles Deputy District Attorney Robin Sax, brings clarity to the issue. With more than fifteen years of experience prosecuting sex crimes against children, Ms. Sax is an acknowledged authority on child sexual abuse. She categorizes the various aspects of the larger issue by using a logical and easily understood question-and-answer format. We first learn how to recognize predators and child molesters, how to define their actions, and how to respond to their advances. By the end of the book, we are expertly counseled on how to heal and move on. By prioritizing the welfare of the victim, Ms. Sax systematically separates fear from fact and ignorance from knowledge. Her holistic approach to the issue leaves us with a greater understanding as she informs and educates parents about threats real and imagined.

The days of telling your children not to talk to strangers are long gone. We now know that the problem is not stranger-centric. The predator's playground has extended beyond the schoolyard. We know that it exists in cyberspace, at church, and even at home. In fact, statistics suggest that 70 to 80 percent of children who are molested are victimized by a family member or somebody that they know. If we are going to protect our children against victimization, recognize it when it exists, and ensure that it can be properly dealt with when it has been established, then society must take advantage of every viable tool that is provided to us. I have no doubt that *Predators and Child Molesters: What Every Parent Needs to Know to Keep Kids Safe* will quickly become an important weapon in the war against sexual predation.

INTRODUCTION

There is no other crime—not even murder—that worries and sickens parents more than child sexual abuse. Part of that fear is related to all the questions parents have that they don't know whom to ask, are too scared to ask, or choose not to deal with. Much of the confusion about how to deal with such abuse arises from the complexities surrounding this growing societal problem.

It's not surprising that parents don't understand either the questions that arise or the problem itself. After all, it wasn't until 2000 that the Department of Justice began recording statistics of sexual assault against children. Even then, there was debate over which definitions of sexual assault would be reported. Would they report only forcible acts? Would these be limited to crimes of penetration?

Only recently are we finally getting a handle on the problem—one far greater than any of us might have imagined.

Since 2000, the Department of Justice and other law enforcement agencies have made protecting children a priority, as seen in our mandatory reporting laws, the formation of special teams to deal with child sexual assault, and the creation of more laws to protect children.

Every day, the government, social action groups, victims, and survivors are working harder than ever to give a voice to our children. The laws are constantly being revised to keep up with changes in societal times and technology. Just look at ABC-TV's popular show *To Catch a Predator*, which broke new ground as it followed predators from every walk of life as they hunted their victims. Society is finally ready to accept that we have a problem keeping our children safe.

We now know that the only way to protect children is for parents to view it as a priority—not once the deed is done, but as a preventive measure. The intention to protect our children should be as natural as teaching them how to call 9-1-1.

Protecting children begins with every parent in every home. It is the parents' responsibility to partner with schools to teach their children how to be safe. And how do they do that? By asking tough questions and demanding straight answers.

After fifteen years as a prosecutor, I get asked the same questions every day. They come up whether I am in the office, in court, giving a lecture, or talking to other moms. Inevitably one question leads to another, then the floodgates are open and more questions pour out. There are always the same concerns: What is sexual assault anyway? How do I know if my child has been touched? Wouldn't my child tell me? What happens if I report it?

Have you noticed that sexual assault hits the news more and more often? High-profile teachers are hauled into court; actors are arrested; protracted abuse and kidnappings are suddenly revealed, such as the case of an Austrian man who abused his daughter for twenty-four years, keeping her hidden in a cellar all that time.

Sensationalism may be swirling around you, but what about all the other cases that don't make headlines? What about the hundred thousand child abuse allegations reported every year by "regular people" each day?

In this book, I'll tackle the questions parents have asked me about how best to protect their kids from predators and abusers. The answers may surprise you. They will definitely enlighten you. And that's my hope in writing this book— to help you create the safest environment for your kids and prevent them from becoming a predator's next victim.

AUTHOR'S NOTE

I write this book from the perspective of a lawyer. While the job of a prosecutor crosses over to some other disciplines, like advocate, therapist, social worker, and police officer, my job is very much about what is legal and illegal, what will and will not hold up in court, and what the criminal process will do for the victim and perpetrator.

Therefore, as you read my answers to these questions, I highlight and discuss the law, as well as the policy behind the law, so that you can see why I am answering a question in a particular way.

The information in this book will indicate the different roles and perspectives of the variety of professionals involved in child sexual assault. However, since I am the prosecuting attorney, keep in mind that I will always have one eye focused on the law—and what works in court.

This book is not intended to supply legal advice. This book is meant to provide information and insights based on my years of experience in criminal justice. Since laws vary from state to state and change from year to year, be sure to consult an attorney to make any decisions regarding your legal rights and responsibilities.

And one more legal caveat, this book is written by me as an individual and does not represent the opinions or views of the Los Angeles County District Attorney, the District Attorney's Office, or Los Angeles County as a whole.

Now, a word about gender. As politically correct as I try to be, the reality is that most perpetrators are men and most victims are female. That is not to say that there are not male victims or female perpetrators. In order to streamline this book, I take on the statistical approach and refer to perps as "he" and victims as "she."

PART ONE

RECOGNIZING THE PREDATORS
Molesters, Pedophiles, and Opportunists

QUESTION 1: HOW PREVALENT IS CHILD SEXUAL ABUSE?

This is an excellent question. Because child sexual abuse is underreported, in terms of both victim disclosures and reliable data about offenders, it's challenging to pinpoint the exact number of child sexual assaults. The following are just a few problems in obtaining accurate numbers of sexual abuse cases:

1. The largest bulk of statistics available are from criminal cases. And since we are limited to only the legal definitions of sexual abuse (as I will explore in question 2), we may be missing out on behavior that would otherwise qualify on a psychological or sociological basis.

2. Even under each state's criminal laws, there's a variation in the acts and behaviors that are considered criminal. If an act is not a crime in one place and it is in another, it may not make its way into a statistical information bank.

3. Individual police departments have not had uniform statistics readily accessible to those seeking them. Until the Department of Justice began collecting statistics from police stations across the country, the numbers were all over the place. In fact, even when the statistics became uniform

in the last twenty years or so, only certain specific acts were identified and reported, including forcible rape, forcible sodomy, sexual assault with an object, and forcible fondling. These statistics do not take into account the many other acts, such as photographing children in sexual situations, that could still be subject to criminal charges, be considered sexual abuse, or cause psychological damage in someone's life.

4. If we were to look at child sexual assault from other avenues, such as from the offenders or the victims themselves, there are new problems in gathering information. First of all, offenders traditionally offer unreliable information about their offenses. If we turn to the victims, we find difficulty due to their reluctance to disclose what actually happened, memory lapses, and the reality that victims are often molested by more than one person during their lives, or at a specific time and place.

5. False allegations of child abuse occur when people disclose child sexual assault when it didn't happen. Not only does this affect the reliability of the statistics, but this is one of the biggest points of controversy and concern in the field because it creates the potential for heavily biased or inaccurate data.

6. Perhaps the biggest reason is that victims, quite understandably, are loathe to report that they have been abused. As I discuss in more detail in question 46, there are so many reasons why children don't report (shame, guilt, lack of knowledge, etc.) that even the professionals don't have a full grasp of the extent of the problem.

Despite the problem of variance in reporting child sexual assaults, there are considerable data that confirm my experience that child sexual assault is rampant.

In 2007, FBI reports revealed that:

- One out of five girls will be sexually molested before her eighteenth birthday.
- One out of six boys will be sexually molested before his eighteenth birthday.
- One out of every seven victims of sexual assault reported to law enforcement agencies was under age six.
- Forty percent of the offenders who victimized children under age six were juveniles (under eighteen).

- Two out of three sexual abuses are perpetrated against teenagers or younger children.
- Twenty percent of all children receive unwanted sexual messages.
- Seventy-five percent of children who received an unwanted sexual message did not tell their parents.
- Four million kids are posting on the Web every day.
- There are four hundred thousand new victims of sexual assault each year.
- There are more than 550,000 registered sex offenders in the United States.
- There are more than a hundred thousand sex offenders who fail to register each year.
- Seventy-six percent of serial rapists claim they were molested as children.
- Over forty percent of male juvenile delinquents were molested as children.

Perhaps the single most disturbing statistic I have come across is a study done by Dr. Gene Abel in the late 1980s on sexual offenders. In his research, he found that there was only a three percent chance of an offender getting caught for a sexual offense. Because of the problems mentioned above in reporting these crimes, Dr. Abel's statistic hasn't changed significantly over the past twenty-eight years—a damning testimonial to the continuing problem facing everyone who wants to prevent and solve these crimes.

QUESTION 2: HOW DO YOU DEFINE CHILD SEXUAL ABUSE?

There is no single definition of child sexual abuse. The term takes on different meanings depending on who's defining it—psychologists, cops, lawyers, and even victims, survivors, and perpetrators. Legal experts define child sexual abuse as "any act that violates the penal code." Psychologists define it as "any act in which an adult takes advantage of a child for sexual gratification."

Generally, child sexual abuse includes acts and behavior that violate an adult's position of trust and authority by taking advantage of a child's innocence. There is no specific physical act to qualify as sexual assault—in fact, nonphysical acts and behavior can also qualify as sexual abuse of a child. For example, such acts as voyeurism, taking pictures of a child, showing pornography to a child, watching a child undress, or even asking children to touch themselves or others can be considered child sexual abuse. Such acts as instructing a child to masturbate, touching genital areas, oral copulation, penetration, intercourse, and sodomy are the most obvious forms of sexual abuse.

For an act or behavior to be child sexual abuse, both of the following must be in play:

1. a person who is an adult *or* is significantly older *or* occupies a position of trust
2. uses a child for sexual stimulation

As you can see, a specific type of act, kind of force, or lack of consent must be present for an act to be considered child sexual assault. Agreeing to engage in such an act is legally referred to as "consent." Under the law, children do not have the legal capacity to consent unless they are over age eighteen. (In some states the age of consent is sixteen or seventeen.)

While a child's acquiescence may play a role in how people perceive the acts, everyone needs to be aware that the only reason a child is targeted is that an adult wishes to use his or her power, authority, or control to direct sexual acts involving a child to satisfy sexual desires. Often, the child depends on the adult in some way, whether for care, nurturing, education, shelter, and so forth, and feels his or her life could be in jeopardy by resisting the adult's wishes.

There are three forms of child sexual abuse:

1. Sexual assault: The focus of sexual assault is the physical component of the abuse. This is all the physical acts, including rape, sodomy, sexual penetration, oral copulation, digital penetration whether by a finger or other object other than a penis, and other lewd acts where physical contact is used for sexual gratification.
2. Sexual molestation: The focus of sexual molestation is the intent of the perpetrator to create inappropriate behavior. This includes any act where an adult engages in behavior that is not necessarily physical but uses a child for sexual gratification. Sexual molestation is further broken down into two categories:

A. Situational child molesters: A situational child molester is someone who does not necessarily have a sexual preference or attraction to children but at some point engaged in a sexual act with a child.

Mary Kay Letourneau was the first of the modern female child molesters entrusted to teaching our children. A sixth grade teacher, Mary Kay, although married with children, had sex with her thirteen-year-old male student and served just over seven years in prison as a result. Unable to stay away from the boy, she resumed her relationship with him and went on to produce two children with her teen lover. Later, they were married. Letourneau is considered a situational child molester because it was her unique attraction to the victim, not a general desire to be sexually gratified by children, that landed her in trouble.

B. Preferential child molesters: A preferential child molester is someone with a permanent fixation or desire to be with children. This is a person who is either only sexually attracted to children or is always attracted to children, with adults secondary in appeal. Whereas situational child molesters likely have few victims, and sometimes only one, preferential child molesters usually have many more than are ever known or reported.

3. Sexual exploitation: This occurs when an adult victimizes a child for personal advancement, sexual gratification, and financial profit. Examples of this would be exposing children to pornography, creating and trafficking child pornography, selling children into prostitution rings, and so on.

The term *child sexual offender* refers to anyone who has ultimately been convicted for one or more of the above child sexual offenses.

QUESTION 3: WHAT ARE THE DIFFERENCES BETWEEN A PEDOPHILE, AN OPPORTUNIST, A MOLESTER, AND A PREDATOR?

A number of different terms are used to describe child sexual offenders, depending on who's defining these types and the context of the statement, including *pedophile*, *predator*, *opportunist*, *molester*, *sex offender*, and *incest offender*. That these terms can be used interchangeably is confusing both to victims and society in general. The National Center for Exploitation and Missing Children says it best: "Referring to the same thing by different names and different things by the same name frequently creates confusion." This also affects the disclosures and reporting of sexual impropriety. Parents who don't want to accept an inappropriate situation may pretend it doesn't exist rather than deal with all the fallout from confronting it. However, children must be protected whether or not there's an official definition for inappropriate sexual activity involving a minor.

Regardless of what term is used, it is illegal and inappropriate to touch a child in any way for lewd intent. Further, any act that feels wrong or inappropriate is wrong or inappropriate, period. No matter how kind or upstanding the citizen, or how unfathomable it may be to parents that someone has turned their child's world upside down, there must be the courage—as parents—to confront a situation that feels wrong. As author and security specialist Gavin de Becker so aptly put it, we all benefit when we recognize "the gift of fear" (the title of his best-selling book) and act on it, particularly when the fear begins to haunt our lives or those of our loved ones.

Pedophile

People use the term *pedophile* to describe someone with an unnatural sexual interest in children. The "bible" of psychological conditions, the *Diagnostic and Statistical Manual of Mental Disorders, Fourth Edition*, defines the criteria for pedophilia as follows:

A. The person, over a period of at least 6 months, has a recurrence of intense, sexually arousing fantasies, sexual urges, or behavior involving sexual activity with a prepubescent child or children (generally age 13 years or younger).

B. The person acts on these urges, or they create distress or difficulty in his life.

C. The person is at least age 16 years and at least 5 years older than the child or children in Criterion A.

(Note: This definition does not include an individual in late adolescence involved in an ongoing sexual relationship with a 12- or 13-year-old.)

While the preceding may provide some helpful criteria for evaluating who is a pedophile, criterion B creates some confusion. It states that to be a pedophile, the attraction to children must interfere with one's way of life. But most offenders would probably say that their interests never interfered with their life until their activities were reported to the police! By extension, that would imply that only when caught and possibly convicted would a person be deemed a pedophile. That is the route law enforcement has taken: officially, a pedophile is someone who has been convicted of, or is awaiting charges on, child sexual assault.

However, in most contexts, a pedophile refers to a person who is sexually attracted to and/or has an unnatural sexual interest in children. Merriam-Webster at least simplifies the definition by explaining a pedophile to be a person who has a "sexual perversion in which children are the preferred sexual object." This definition represents the mainstream, societal view of a pedophile—most people have a gut feeling that a pedophile is someone aroused by children.

Noticeably absent from most people's definition of pedophile are acts that are considered "statutory rape" or "unlawful sex." Statutory rape involves circumstances where the law defines a particular sex act as illegal strictly based on the victim's age. These acts are consensual and generally lack the perversity and grotesqueness of the traditional sexual assault acts. Statutory rapes present a lot of issues for parents, psychologists, and prosecutors because, again, there is a wide variety of what can technically qualify as statutory rape.

For example, under California law, statutory rape can be consensual sex between a fifteen-year-old and a twenty–year-old or consensual sex between a sixteen-year-old and a fifty-year-old. Certainly, parents, prosecutors, and psychologists have concern for the well-being of a sixteen-year-old who believes that he or she is in love and having a consensual relationship with a fifty-year-old.

Opportunist

The debate as to who exactly qualifies as a pedophile has given rise to other categories of offenders. Opportunists are a prime example. Some researchers and social scientists believe that pedophiles can be sexually attracted only to children. Therefore, people who sexually abuse a child and still maintain an interest in sex with people their own ages are placed in another category of offender called *opportunists*.

The definition of *opportunist* is related to the perpetrator's motivation, but not necessarily the act. For example, a thirty-year-old who has sex with a twelve-year-old could be called an opportunist or a pedophile, depending on whether the act was a one-time isolated incident (opportunist) or whether there is a consistent, ongoing preference or fixation for children (pedophile).

One specific category of opportunist is the incest offender. These abusers molest only their own children. Are they simply "lazy" offenders who molest the children most accessible to them—their own? Which leads to the question: Are these offenders really only attracted to their own kids or would they also seek other children to molest if they did not have their own or if their own were unavailable?

Molester

A molester is someone who touches a child in a sexual way that is unlawful but does not involve penetration. The offending act is done by an adult, male or female, against a minor that causes the adult to be aroused or excited.

The most common acts include the touching and fondling of a child. Legally, any touching or fondling does not need to be at skin level—it may also include the child's clothes or any protective layering. The law focuses on the intent of the individual, which may explain why touching can be of clothing as well as skin.

Some people will define molestation to include one's normal sexual activities, such as vaginal intercourse or oral copulation. For our purposes, molestation is a nonpenetrative act, while sexual abuse is a penetrative act. In addition, acts that include the flashing of the genitals, showing of pornography or sexually explicit materials, and deviant sexual activities (defecation, urination, bondage) are all considered to be molesting acts.

Furthermore, the law is very clear that a child's consent is not a defense for adults who molest children who are under a certain age (which varies from state to state). Therefore, even if a minor had given permission for the adult to touch him or her, it is still illegal. The rationale behind the denial of consent as a defense for molesters is that the child-adult relationship is considered affected by the adult's power and influence over a child's decisions. I will discuss consent in more detail in question 5.

Predator

Predator is a term that doesn't look at the acts or motivation behind child sexual abuse; rather, it is a term of numbers. A person who has assaulted either the same person or several people is called a predator. It's a common misperception that those who have sexually abused children are automatically predators because of the strong belief that predators are impossible to rehabilitate. Some states have set forth specific "sexually violent predators" acts or laws, which allow officials to keep individuals in prison even longer than their original sentence if they qualify as a continued threat to the public.

Throughout this book, I use these terms based on how society has come to use them.

- A *pedophile* is the psychiatric medical term for someone who has a sexual attraction to and preference for children. It is important to note that just because a pedophile prefers children does not necessarily mean that he never has sexual relationships with adults.
- An *opportunist* is a type of pedophile who may have acted only when the circumstance presented itself. The act was not a normal aspect of his or her regular sexual proclivities.
- A *molester* is the criminal term for someone who has acted out sexually against a child, whether the behavior was based on pedophilia, attraction, or any other motivation.
- The term *incest offender* can be used interchangeably to define pedophiles who molest their own children.
- A *predator* is a pedophile who has offended more than one time.

QUESTION 4: WHAT ACTS ARE CONSIDERED SEXUALLY ABUSIVE?

Under most state laws, sexually abusive acts include, but are not limited to, rape, statutory rape, incest, sodomy, lewd and lascivious acts against minors, oral copulation, sexual penetration, and child molestation. In fact, any touching that has an aura of sexuality, regardless of location of the touch or the motivation behind it, can be considered sexually abusive behavior.

When determining which acts are sexually abusive, it is important to separate those that are wrong and inappropriate but may not necessarily qualify as a crime to be charged by a prosecutor. (In question 73, I discuss which specific acts translate into criminal charges.) However, the easiest test of whether an act is abusive is this: "If it feels wrong to the recipient, then it is wrong."

Any act, behavior, comment, or direction that is sexual in nature and is meant to stimulate either the perpetrator or the child victim is sexually abusive. The range of acts is huge. On one end of the spectrum are rape and sodomy and on the other are certain gestures and comments; of course, there are many more in between.

To get a sense of what is clearly sexually abusive, states' penal codes are very clear. I believe that when parents (and children) see that an action is actually against the law, they are then more willing to accept that it might actually be abusive. Therefore, let's look to the law for guidance, recognizing that other behaviors that are not necessarily criminal or provable can still be considered sexual abuse.

- *Lewd and lascivious acts:* This describes any sexual touching (not even necessarily on a child's private area) of a child under a specific age defined by the state. For example, in California, the age is fourteen, while in Florida, the age is sixteen.
- *Rape:* Rape occurs when a man penetrates a vagina (regardless of the victim's age) with his penis. Usually this is accomplished by force, fear, duress, undue influence, coercion, intoxication, or other reason preventing the victim from consenting—including being under age.
- *Sodomy:* This refers to penetration—no matter how slight—of the anus by a penis.
- *Digital penetration by foreign object:* The vagina or anus is penetrated by something other than a penis.
- *Oral copulation:* This occurs when one person puts his or her mouth on another person's sexual organ.
- *Incest:* A specific blood relationship between sexual partners is incest, which is illegal in most states.
- *Indecent exposure:* Exhibitionists and others who display their genitals in a public place can be charged with indecent exposure.
- *Peeping Tom statutes:* A person, while prowling, loitering, or wandering, "peeks" at someone without his or her knowledge to gratify sexual desires and lust.

- *Soliciting sex with a minor:* This occurs when an adult requests someone under the legal age of consent to have sex. Frequently, a solicitation happens on the Internet but can also occur on the phone or in person.
- *Child pornography:* Laws pertaining to child pornography range from simple possession of child pornography, to mailing or e-mailing pornography to a child, to selling child pornography.
- *Pimping and pandering:* This refers to earning money or proceeds from the prostitution of others.

QUESTION 5: IF THE CHILD CONSENTS, IS IT CONSIDERED SEXUAL ABUSE?

Every single state has adopted laws that affirm that children of a certain age do not have the legal capacity to consent to any type of sexual contact. What that magic number is varies from state to state, generally ranging between sixteen and eighteen.

While actual birth age is one factor in the ability to consent, many states also have adopted "functional age" or "mental age" equivalents. They presume that people who are mentally or emotionally deficient lack the ability to make clear judgments about such requests for sex and can be taken advantage of by such predators.

"Consent" implies that both parties possess equal power and authority. Just as a child cannot sign a legally binding contract, a child cannot give legal consent to sexual activity. The laws of consent are rooted in the fact that adults often exploit children. In addition, sometimes young people do not have the ability to make well-thought-out decisions. They may not truly appreciate the nature and the consequences of their actions. With sex acts in particular, many children can end up pregnant, subject to disease, or fall prey to other adverse consequences.

Some states have identified certain ages that are incontestable regarding a child's ability to give consent. The child is presumed unable to consent regardless of the age difference between the perpetrator and the victim, the nature of the relationship, or how the child may feel about the circumstances. The cutoff for most states is age fourteen. In cases where the children are between fourteen and seventeen, some states will factor in the age difference between the alleged perpetrator and the victim to determine if there is sexual abuse as defined by criminal codes.

Although children really cannot, under the law, consent, it is a real factor that people will consider in deciding how to handle these cases. For example, it is a very different situation when a twenty-year-old has sex with a ten-year-old versus the same twenty-year-old having sex with a sixteen-year-old, even if both are supposedly consensual.

Under most state laws, consent is defined as "the positive cooperation by both parties where both people can appreciate both the nature of the act and the consequences of the acts they are agreeing to." *Positive cooperation* indicates a non-forcing of the participants, a willingness not influenced by fear, duress, or illegal substances.

QUESTION 6: HOW PREVALENT IS SEXUAL ABUSE OF MALES?

Sexual abuse of boys is vastly understudied, underreported, and misunderstood. According to the Rape Abuse Incest National Network (RAINN), 2.78 million men have been victims of sexual assault in the United States. Further, about three percent of American men—or one in thirty-three—have experienced an attempted or a completed rape in their lifetime.

While many of the same issues exist in sexual abuse of females, there is a whole range of other issues that arise when dealing with sexual assault of males. The most common myths include:

1. "Most sexual assaults of males are perpetrated by homosexual males." Perhaps one of the most difficult aspects of reporting for boys who are molested is the fear that they will be perceived as a homosexual or that they will "turn gay" due to the abuse. Sexual assault is not about sexual preference. While many child molesters have gender and/or age preferences, of those who seek out boys, the vast majority are not homosexual. They are pedophiles.
2. "Sexual assaults by females deserve a 'high five.'" There is a widespread belief that boys who are initiated into sexual activity by a female should consider themselves lucky. Society has generally supported the belief that a boy who enters into a heterosexual relationship—regardless of his

or the perpetrator's age—is simply undergoing a rite of passage. The reality is that sexual assault of a minor has the same damaging effects for boys and girls. It is coercing children to engage in an activity that they are not physically, mentally, or developmentally able to understand, appreciate, or consent to.

3. "Boys should be strong about sexual assault, not 'wimp out' and show emotion." This perception makes the chances of disclosure and therefore help and recovery even lower for boys than for girls.

Most people simply cannot wrap their minds around the concept that a male can be a victim of sexual assault. Often, people want to believe that boys are victim-proof—that is, able to protect themselves—and therefore not vulnerable. In truth, boys are children, just like girls. They are just as weak, subject to the same pressures, and always more vulnerable than their perpetrators.

As in all sexual assault generally, the perpetrator exercises power and control over the boy to take advantage of him for sexual purposes. Both boys and girls, and men and women, deserve equal support, sympathy, and a chance to prosecute their abusers.

QUESTION 7: ARE "PEEPING TOMS" AND PEOPLE WHO EXPOSE THEMSELVES CONSIDERED SEX OFFENDERS?

Peeping Toms

There is a whole group of sex offenders out there known as *voyeurs*, including Peeping Toms, exhibitionists, and indecent exposers. On the sex offense continuum, these are perceived as relatively minor, as there is no victim who has been touched.

A Peeping Tom is a person who looks through a window or any other opening while another person is undressing or engaging in intercourse. Laws that criminalize Peeping Tom behavior vary from state to state. Many states do not specifically have Peeping Tom laws but characterize this behavior as an invasion of privacy, disorderly conduct, or trespassing. In most states, Peeping Tom behavior is a misdemeanor, punishable by up to one year in jail and a thousand dollar fine. These people are not required to register as sex offenders, although many debate whether the public should treat them as sex offenders, even though the law does not.

Sometimes, a Peeping Tom will use a videotape to film people undressing; they might also use a two-way mirror to sneak a peek at their targets. These behaviors suggest that planning is involved. When the target is a child, there should be considerable concern.

Many people find it frustrating that it is hard to prosecute Peeping Tom cases successfully, many people try to obtain financial compensation or punishment from these perpetrators through a civil court action. Unfortunately, many of them have no resources to pay for any judgments, and the victim is left with no legal or economic recourse. However, for perpetrators who do have money, victims recover damages by describing the emotional and psychological distress they have suffered as a result of the Peeping Tom experience.

The loose laws pertaining to Peeping Toms make it harder for parents to protect their children because Peeping Toms can continue their activities without fear of a long jail term. The best thing for parents to do is to tell their children to always close their blinds before they change or go to sleep, make sure a trusted adult accompanies the child to a dressing room, and always keep an eye out for suspicious people and suspicious behavior. Parents should also be familiar with their neighbors and note whether there is an intuitive feeling that a neighbor poses a risk.

Exposers

People who expose themselves may be considered sex offenders. In many states, such as California, the flashing of a breast or the exposure of one's genitals may be sufficient to constitute a sex crime. The biggest factors in determining whether exposure is considered a sex crime are location and intent. People who get sexually aroused by exposing themselves have a condition called paraphilia. This sexual desire is not culturally normal, and it's considered a mental disorder. Just like Peeping Toms, people who engage in paraphilia have abnormal ways of expressing their sexual desires. They cross the line of acceptable behavior by invading others' privacy and shocking people who come into contact with them.

Because indecent exposure is considered a sexual offense of sorts, states like California will require a person convicted of this crime to register as a sex offender even if only prosecuted as a lower-level misdemeanor as opposed to a felony.

Indecent exposure, Peeping Toms, prostitution, and even loitering can be behavior that should raise parents' and other caretakers' antennae as a warning sign that a person may be a predator or a pedophile. Like the use of drugs beginning with alcohol and marijuana and then increasing to more serious drugs, sexual assault may begin with voyeurism and then progress to more serious behavior.

QUESTION 8: WHAT IS MEGAN'S LAW?

Megan's Law, named after Megan Nicole Kanka, is the law that requires sex offenders to provide certain information to the law enforcement agency nearest their homes. This is known as *sex offender registration*. This law is intended to help track sex offenders—it is not intended to be a source of punishment for the offender.

While each state has its own requirements as to exactly what information an offender must provide, the purpose of the law is consistent from state to state—to monitor the location of sex offenders. Some states focus on sex offenders as a whole, equally treating those convicted of any sex-related crime, whether against an adult or a child. Other states require registration only by those convicted of child-related sex crimes. The federal version of the same law is known as "The Sexual Offender (Jacob Wetterling) Act of 1994." Under federal law, anyone convicted of child sexual assault must notify their local law enforcement of their whereabouts after being released from jail, prison, a psychiatric institution, or a treatment facility.

The theory behind Megan's Law is that anonymous sex offenders pose risks to society. Megan's parents found this out firsthand when, in 1994, a neighbor lured their seven-year-old daughter into his house, sexually abused her, then murdered her. That neighbor had been previously convicted and served time in prison for aggravated assault and attempted sexual assault.

Sex offenders have a higher rate of recidivism (re-arrest for the same kind of crime) than those convicted of any other offense. One of the most extensive studies ever conducted was done by the Department of Justice in 1994. The results showed that, "compared to non-sex offenders released from State prisons, released sex offenders were four times more likely to be rearrested for a sex crime." With these statistics and their personal experience to support it, the Kanka family helped initiate laws requiring some form of sex offender registration in every state. Their belief is summarized in their mission statement: "Every parent should have the right to know if a dangerous sexual predator moves into their neighborhood."

As with many other laws, some people support Megan's Law and some don't. Its defenders believe that disclosing personal information allows the public to monitor and track sex offenders, helping parents protect their children. The law also helps law enforcers who are investigating sex crimes know the whereabouts of previous offenders.

Opponents of Megan's Law feel it is too invasive and a violation of privacy rights, setting people up for being the outcasts and victims of society's vigilantes. One of the strongest arguments disfavoring Megan's Law is the retroactive application of it. Under retroactivity, even people who were convicted of a sexual offense prior to the passage of a state's version of the law still need to register under the current Megan's Law. This means that if a person previously pled guilty, theoretically he or she must suffer this consequence without being made aware of it in advance.

Registration remains legal as courts have found that the rational basis for the law outweighs the limitations on one's individual liberty and rights. People would rather protect and inform parents and children, even at the cost of minor infringement on personal rights.

In most states, information about registrants under Megan's Law can be accessed online. By typing in an address at a particular location, anyone can see the identity of sex offenders living in their vicinity. Usually included in the Web site's database is the name of the person, the offender's address, and the sex crimes for which the offender was convicted.

As a parent, I suggest that you check whether any sex offenders reside near your home, your school, grandparents' homes, and other locations where your kids frequently hang out. Be sure to share that information with co-parents, babysitters, nannies, grandparents, caretakers, and anyone else responsible for supervising and caring for your children. You should also print out a photo so local sex offenders can be recognized. (I do not recommend sharing the specifics of who may be a sex offender with young children. Simply continue to review how children can keep themselves safe when they're out of your sight.)

QUESTION 9: WHAT DOES A MOLESTER LOOK LIKE?

Sexual abusers (whether pedophiles, predators, or molesters) come from all ethnic and socioeconomic backgrounds. Although there are no consistent physical or psychological traits to help you identify a molester, some general observations can alert a parent to what to look for:

1. Sexual abusers generally have a preexisting relationship with their victims. They have access, authority, and the trust of both the parent and child.
2. Sexual abusers might spend an unusual amount of time with kids, leading observant parents to wonder why they would rather hang around with kids instead of their peers.
3. Often, molesters seek jobs that put them in proximity to and allow for continuous access to children, such as the priesthood or coaching school teams. Or they might find ways to isolate themselves with children when no adults or parents are present, such as at video game centers or malls.
4. Molesters often give suspicious presents or do favors for children. These behaviors are signs of grooming, pay-offs, or guilt gifts. Parents should know where objects come from and why a child received something. For example, unexplained clothes, jewelry, phones, shoes, manicures, and so forth, should be inquired about. Children should be told that they need to ask their parents before receiving any gifts.
5. Bizarre behavior or a "bad vibe" can be a suspicious sign. If something doesn't feel right, this is a possible warning sign of a molester.

While it may be advisable to warn children of "stranger danger," I often remind parents that if they want to worry, they should worry about the people they know as well as the ones they don't. A molester can be a teacher, neighbor, friend, or family member. To assume that we understand the heart and intent of every person in our lives is to turn a blind eye to statistics. These show that molestation occurs more often from people that we know rather than from strangers. Therefore, a molester does not always look "creepy"—in fact, molesters can appear to be warm, caring, loving, and respectful. It is these very characteristics that allow them to continue their horrific acts without the fear of ever being caught.

The idea that a child molester is not off-putting on initial contact is particularly difficult for society to embrace. People prefer to see a molester as someone who has a scary appearance. It's even more difficult when the molester seems to have good qualities, thus making him appear not all bad. In addition, children are rarely seen as completely good—that is, kids can do bad things like lie or cheat or steal—which fuels society's reluctance to accept how prevalent child sexual assault really is. Sometimes people may have a hard time believing kids, such as a rebellious teenager's word against that of a respectable teacher, but parents should think twice. Offenders often pick imperfect victims, knowing that they are less likely to be believed or trusted.

The following findings may surprise you. Studies have shown that common qualities of sexual abusers include rigid religious backgrounds, depression, isolation, inability to relate to adults, and a history of having been abused (neglected or physically or sexually assaulted) themselves. Child molesters often lack social skills, have psychological problems, don't know how to appropriately behave with others, and may believe they have special rights and privileges.

Parents must be aware of child molesters who use their power and status within the family or community to gain a child's trust. For example, teachers are highly regarded and respected. Parents should not blindly assume that every teacher is good-hearted and focused on their child's moral, psychological, and educational development (although most are). In many parts of the country, teachers and clergy have been convicted of repeated child abuse. These unpleasant facts are not intended to attack the integrity of religious and educational institutions. The truth is, most of these institutions are highly professional, honest, and upright. However, being too trustworthy can sometimes put a child in danger. To say that sexual assault doesn't occur in schools, churches, temples, and so on, is as unrealistic as saying that police officers, lawyers, and judges never lie!

QUESTION 10: WHAT IS "GROOMING"?

Grooming is a method by which abusers get victims to comply with their sexual wishes. The grooming process is specifically designed to lull the child into a sense of ease, thus blurring any awareness of improper adult behavior. This is initiated by gaining the child's trust and confidence before any sexual abuse occurs. In fact, at the beginning, the molester will be kind, engage in conversation, show interest, and pay lots of attention to a child. This seemingly innocent behavior is intended to make a child feel comfortable before any hint of sexual inappropriateness begins. Then, the abuser begins to move along a continuum—from seemingly innocent actions through various levels of inappropriate behavior. This slow progression is meant to make the child comfortable with an increasing level of sexuality by the adult.

A predator will use everyday behavior, like telling a sexual joke, touching the child on the upper arm a little too long, or kissing the child on the lips instead of the cheek as a way to test whether the child is likely to tell others. If the perpetrator is satisfied that the child won't tell, other forms of touching will follow. If the child still doesn't tell, then the contact often progresses into more advanced or protracted sexual abuse.

Grooming, like sexual assault, will progress through various phases, each more outrageous than the next. This tactic is used not only on the child victim but often on a parent or caregiver as well, helping accelerate the child's grooming. The predator uses the parents' "blessing" and trust as a way to interpose himself between the child and the parent, as well as to minimize the wrongfulness of the predator's behavior.

Some examples of grooming a parent include gaining trust by always being there, being eager to babysit, being able to help with the kids in a pinch, and offering to give a confused parent insight into the child. In this way, the child's support network is groomed to believe in the predator and to disbelieve anything the child may say later about the predator's behavior. Predators may try to win parents' confidence and support by having some quick conversations about a lie the child told. They may even suggest that there's something not right or unbalanced about the child.

Grooming is easiest when there is some sort of preexisting relationship or connection between the molester and the child. Besides family members, teachers, religious leaders, coaches, and babysitters can also use their knowledge of a child, and the built-up trust and power of their relationship, to successfully groom a child. Perhaps the most distinctive example of this can be seen in the Catholic Church's recent abuse cases. Over five thousand priests used their relationships with both child victims and parents to gain trust, access, and secrecy in order to abuse children.

QUESTION 11: WHERE DO MOLESTERS SEEK THEIR VICTIMS?

Molestation does not occur in any specific place; it occurs primarily when the following two elements exist: access and privacy.

Access

Predators seek opportunities and look for openings to be with children, such as a career choice, a living arrangement, or an offer to "help" single-parent friends. As a parent, I would never volunteer to babysit just any kid; it would have to be for some darn good reason. Parents should ask themselves, why is this person willing (or even wanting) to spend so much time with my child?

Experienced predators find ways to get close to children without arousing suspicion. Predators are adept in creating situations where they can spend time alone with a child. For example, a teacher may offer a child after-school tutoring or give him a ride home, or a neighbor may pay a teenager to do yard work as a way to get him inside the home.

Privacy

Typically, predators seek places where the number of potential witnesses, corroborating evidence, and chances of discovery are low. These are areas that are usually difficult for other people to access (e.g., cars, homes, locked rooms). Here, the predator and the victim are the only witnesses to the crime, and the victim will have difficulty getting help. Predators also seek places where the victim would be likely to get in trouble if parents knew that he or she was there. For example, a child at someone's house during the middle of the school day is less likely to disclose the abuse for fear of punishment for missing a class.

One key issue I see in trials is the jury's desire to hear from people who have actually seen the crime—"eyewitnesses." And while eyewitnesses and videotapes would be ideal, they rarely turn up to clarify what happened in a crime, let alone a sex crime. Why is that? Most criminals (and noncriminals) are savvy enough to realize that it is better not to commit a crime where they will get caught. So criminals will go to great lengths to ensure that there are no witnesses or, in case of a stranger, to disguise himself. Since the victim in a sexual assault case is clearly a witness, the perpetrator can turn to a number of measures to "take care" of that witness. The best way is to use all the dirt that the predator knows from grooming to dirty the credibility of the victim.

Besides the fact that a crime is usually committed in privacy, there is an extra layer of privacy in sexual assault—after all, sex, by its nature, is extremely private. Sex, even between consenting adults, is something that most people don't discuss with others. The dangerous mix of access and privacy creates a circumstance that supports the act of sexual abuse—and creates an environment in which the victim is less likely to disclose the deed.

QUESTION 12: WHY ARE CHILDREN SUSCEPTIBLE TO SEXUAL ABUSE?

There is a vulnerability about children that makes them "perfect victims" for sexual abuse. Children are usually poor witnesses and easy targets for sexual abuse. Other reasons why children are prime candidates for sexual assault include:

1. There are certain expectations about the relationship between children and adults.
   - Children are taught to trust adults.
   - Children depend on adults.
   - Children are raised to respect elders.
   - Children are taught that adults are authority figures.
2. Children are attracted to new experiences and experimentation.
   - Children are curious.
   - Children are willing to experiment and test new grounds.
   - Children, especially teenagers, are defiant.
   - Children tend to engage in more risk-taking behavior.
   - Children crave attention.
   - Children crave affection.
3. Children make poor witnesses in court.
   - Juries may not understand children's terms for parts of their bodies or sexual acts.
   - People tend to believe that children are easily suggestible or coached.
   - Children are not as skilled at lying as adults, and their lies are easily spotted, causing doubt regarding their allegations toward adults.

Children with disabilities are potentially at greater risk for abuse. Those who are disabled, whether physically, emotionally, or developmentally, are even more dependent on adults and have even less understanding of their vulnerability to predators and molesters.

As parents, the best we can do is raise assertive, confident children with a higher sense of self-worth and self-esteem. Such children are less likely to be targeted because they are more likely to say "no" to a predator and more likely to report the incident. From the predator's point of view, why take the risk of seducing an assertive child when a weak and meek one will do what the predator wants and keep her mouth shut?

QUESTION 13: WHERE DO MOLESTERS LIVE?

A child molester who has never been convicted of a crime can live anywhere. It is only when a sex crime is reported that he or she even appears on the radar of the public or law enforcement. And it is only after an actual conviction (either by plea or jury verdict) that a child molester is required to register.

Molesters who have been convicted of a sexual offense must register their current address with their local law enforcement. In fourteen states, there are certain restrictions—for example, molesters cannot live within five hundred to a thousand feet of a school or other location that children frequent.

However, most states have no restrictions. To find out where molesters live, parents can go to their law enforcement agency and ask for a list of all local registered sex offenders, or, in some states, they can search online for any sexual offenders living in their area. By law, each state should have a database of all the sexual offenders who have registered in the state.

Child molesters who are intent on molesting again will naturally move to areas where children are present, regardless of any restrictions the state has imposed. In fact, parents may be surprised to learn that many registered sex offenders live just a few blocks from them. To safeguard your kids, your best resource is to look up sexual offenders living in your area. Just knowing where a molester lives is not foolproof—you need to educate your nannies, caregivers, and family members about the registered sex offenders near home and other often visited places (e.g., school, grandparents' home).

By taking a proactive approach, parents can minimize the danger an offender poses. Many law enforcement Web sites have data on offenders, including their last known address and photograph. This picture should be printed out and placed in an area of the house where everyone can access it. Since younger children should always be supervised, they do not need to be told who the predators are. Older children (twelve and up), who may be permitted to walk around the neighborhood unsupervised, should be told the identities of registered sex offenders. (A factor in deciding whether your child should be unsupervised is whether there are registered sex offenders in an area where you'd normally allow your child to frequent.) Parents also need to take extra precautions when their children are out of their area of influence, ensuring that their children are always surrounded and protected by a person they can truly trust.

While some states require only child molesters to register, a growing number of states require registration of adult sex crime offenders as well. These include those convicted of forcible rape, sodomy, and forcible oral copulation. It is important to remember that any convicted sex offender is dangerous to children. In fact, psychologists have found that, more than any other type of criminal, perpetrators of sex crimes are likely to have a propensity to commit future acts.

In addition, many molesters live among us who are not registered or have never been identified. A recent study by the organization Stop It Now! found that eighty-four percent of sex offenders are "out of registration compliance," which can mean never registered to begin with or the registrant has not kept up with his annual reregistration requirement. The result is that molesters and predators can live anywhere and also be unaccounted for in law enforcement databases.

So how can we find the unidentified or unreported predators? There is no simple answer. All we can do is be aware that child molesters show up wherever they can target and groom their next victim. (See question 16 for tips on protecting your children.)

QUESTION 14: WHY DO PEOPLE MOLEST?

Since there is no uniform profile of a molester, predator, or pedophile, there is no single explanation why people molest.

Molesters will try to convince others that they are people who nurture, understand, and care for children. They will explain that they want to save kids from neglect, unpopularity, and a variety of other supposed problems. The problem is that the predator, while acting kindly, is preparing via grooming his next victim for sexual exploitation.

Some traits associated with child molesters include:

- a history of having been abused as children—physically, verbally, as well as neglect
- depression
- poor impulse control
- repression as a result of rigidly imposed sexual or religious values
- the inability to relate to adults, difficulty empathizing with others—particularly a victim
- isolated from other children at a young age
- poor social skills
- a history of drug or alcohol abuse
- unusual patterns of sexual arousal
- believing he or she is special and entitled to unusual favors
- unhealthy thought patterns that encourage the abuse to continue
- an obsessive need for control

The bottom line that at the root of every molester is a person with a serious psychological condition who is a danger to children anytime and anywhere.

QUESTION 15: WHAT IS THE RELATIONSHIP BETWEEN PORNOGRAPHY AND CHILD MOLESTATION?

Although many factors can lead to an assault, there is a great debate as to whether pornography should be included. Recent studies demonstrate that those who collect and disseminate child pornography are likely to actually molest a child. According to the United States Postal Inspection Service, at least eighty percent of purchasers of child pornography are active child abusers, and nearly forty percent of the child pornographers investigated over the past several years have sexually molested children in the past.

Thus, it is no wonder that parents are concerned about the relationship between pornography and sexual abuse. Pornography can facilitate child molestation in ways other than just stimulating the perpetrator:

1. As an aid to grooming—a sexual predator often uses pornography to lower the victim's inhibitions and to make sexual activity seem perfectly normal.
2. It indicates to a victim what a perpetrator wants to do to a child.
3. It introduces children prematurely to sexual sensations that they are unable to deal with and allows the abuser to take advantage of the resulting guilt and shame.
4. Depending on the type of pornography, it may trivialize women, abuse, or behavior that would otherwise be criminal.

Data gathered from law enforcement investigations conclude that child molesters often collect child pornography. The term *collection* goes beyond mere viewing—it includes systematic saving, categorizing, and fantasizing about the pornographic images According to "Stopping Child Pornography: Protecting our Children and the Constitution: Before the Senate Comm. On the Judiciary, 107th Cong. (2002)" (statement of Ernie Allen, Director, National Center for Missing and Exploited Children), viewing child pornography reinforces fantasies and drives the predator toward acting them out. Therefore, even if an individual is not actively molesting at the time he is investigated for possessing child pornography, an extensive collection indicates his sexual preference for children and is a red flag for possible plans to molest.

It is already well established that the Internet is a powerful tool used by pedophiles and sexual predators to distribute child pornography, engage in sexually explicit conversations with children, and seek victims in chat rooms. The more pornography these individuals access, the higher the risk of their acting out on what they see, including sexual assault, rape, and child molestation.

A pedophile's pornography and erotica collection is the single best indicator of what he wants to do. Perpetrators should be pursued with vigilance, based on the assumption that where there is child pornography, there is most likely child sexual abuse.

PART TWO.

TALKING TO KIDS ABOUT RISKS AND RECOGNIZING POTENTIAL PROBLEMS

QUESTION 16: HOW OFTEN SHOULD I TALK TO MY CHILDREN ABOUT PREVENTING SEXUAL ABUSE?

Two types of safety education work well for parents and children and can easily be added to a family's safety plans: pre-planned discussions and spontaneous opportunities to teach. The first focuses on a particular issue and reinforces it over a period of time, say over a couple weeks to a month. For example, an appropriate safety lesson for a family with young children (ages five and younger) is to help them memorize key telephone numbers, such as Mom's cell, the home phone, and grandparents' or caregivers' numbers. Without making it obvious that it's a safety lesson, teaching a child a telephone number can be made into a song or a game and can be easily practiced.

There is no magic age to begin safety discussions. They should be part of your parenting as soon as your child can understand what you're talking about. The only aspect that will change over time will be the level of discussion. For example, let's take a discussion about getting a "bad vibe" from someone. If you're talking about this with a young child, you'd use language like "people who make you feel yucky." Discussions about "going to get a grown-up before you answer the door," which would be appropriate for a young child, can be changed to "how to answer the door" for an older child.

While actual sit-down conversations that deal with safety may be necessary only every few weeks to once a month, there are countless opportunities for spontaneous discussions and other techniques to reinforce prior lessons. For example, at least once a week when I come home from work, I simply ring the doorbell to see what my daughter (and my nanny) will do when someone comes to the door. The results give me peace of mind as I see that what I've taught them is actually sinking in. It also gives me the opportunity to tweak our family safety discussions based on their response. And of course, I am assessing how well my daughter's nanny responds, so I can be confident that she's providing the supervision I expect.

Parents should make a family rule: "Don't answer the door unless it is Mommy, Daddy, or [a very short list of adults]." The reason is that sometimes certain people are welcome in our homes and sometimes they are not. For example, the plumber whom a child knows may be welcome when there is a plumbing emergency but would not be welcome to just drop by and say hello without notice or permission.

Parents can also include personal safety suggestions at other times and use real-life opportunities to reinforce them. For example, a week before a family vacation to Disneyland is a logical time to discuss what your children would do if they got lost and to talk about "stranger danger." Then, when you arrive at the park, you can make a safety plan consistent with what you'd discussed a few weeks earlier. If you let the kids participate, they can feel a sense of ownership, which encourages them to follow the plan. You can point out meeting places, whom to call for help, and what they should do if they get lost.

Spontaneous teaching moments come up every day and offer opportunities to explore the idea of safety. For instance, if you're crossing the street and see a homeless person begging for money, don't simply walk faster, urging your child to keep going. Instead, ask, "Does that person make you uncomfortable?" If the answer is yes, ask, "Why?" You can then talk about asking for money and switch the scenario: "Well, what do you do if someone isn't asking you for something but instead is *offering* you money, candy, or a gift?" Or you can discuss the "uh-oh" feeling that the homeless person may have triggered so the child can begin to find his or her inner "uh-oh," a warning that something doesn't feel right.

We must remember that we are our children's most important teachers. Kids watch every move we make, question our choices, and observe the results of our actions. We must be sure that we are walking the walk, talking the talk, and not giving mixed messages. For example, it is inconsistent to teach our children not to talk to strangers then at the grocery store tell them, "Say hi to the nice cashier" (who is a stranger). Instead of using stock, outdated one-liners, we need to teach children how to interact safely, recognize potentially dangerous situations, and give them the tools to escape them.

One lesson parents must teach children is the anatomically correct name for their body parts. While many parents call penises "wieners" and breasts "boobies," there are literally hundreds of nicknames that vary from culture to culture and area to area. It is very difficult to ascertain the validity and the details of a sexual assault disclosure if the body-part names used are not familiar to those taking the police report. Once, I had a child that called her vagina "pan." (*Pan* means bread in Spanish.) She kept repeating, "He touched my pan, my pan." And I thought, "He touched your bread?" Fortunately, I had a diagram that the child could look at. But if I were a teacher in the middle of a busy class or a parent making dinner, "He touched my pan" may not register as a disclosure of child sexual assault.

QUESTION 17: HOW CAN I TEACH MY KIDS ABOUT PERSONAL SAFETY WITHOUT SCARING THEM?

The key to keeping such talks from being scary is for parents to assume that body/personal safety discussions are *not* scary. Just because we, as adults, have myriad worries, we needn't convey our fears to our children. However, there are things kids must know before they dive into the world of independent adults.

Just start the discussion. It's never too early to begin to give children information that can help them stay safe. Treat personal safety like any other parenting lesson—find appropriate times, don't tackle too much at a time, and consider the child's personal development and understanding. And above all, do not use fear or scare tactics to educate children. This can often backfire. Empowering, not scaring, children is what allows them to handle the situation, while fear tends to make them freeze and may actually disable them if they need to act in an emergency. The only thing that should scare you is *not* teaching or talking to your children about personal safety.

As trite and overused as the expression seems, knowledge truly is power. I am not suggesting that parents need to tell kids about the gruesome details of every case in the news or drill their kids with statistics. But youngsters need to have a solid understanding of how they can defend themselves in age-appropriate ways. For example, children should know whom to approach if lost in a store (another mommy) or what to scream if someone is trying to abduct them ("You are not my dad! Help!")

The following chart represents the safety issues that must be addressed. While I have designated age groups for some teaching points, it is essential that each age group be covered properly before moving onto the next.

Teaching Points	3–5-Year-Olds	6–11-Year-Olds	12–17-Year-Olds
Your body is your own.	1. Know the names of the body parts. 2. Distinguish between good touches and bad touches. 3. You can say no, "That's not OK," or "Don't touch me "there.	1. You can set limits on who touches you. 2. You have the right to say no to something that makes you feel uncomfortable 3. Some touching is against the law.	1. You deserve to be respected. 2. It's OK to tell someone to stop if you feel disrespeced. It's also OK to leave. 3. Showing affection between an adult and a child does not include touching or kissing private parts, undressing, watching pornography, or having intercourse.
Secrets:	Tell your mom or dad if someone has asked you to keep a secret.	1. Adults should never ask kids to keep a secret. 2. You won't get in trouble for telling your mom or dad any secrets from other adults.	Mom and Dad will believe you if you tell them the secret. Responsible adults don't ask kids to keep secrets
Say no to gifts, candy, or bribes.	You can say no to candy, gifts, or anything without asking a parent first.	You can say no to and *report* bribes.	
Listen to your inner voice and trust your instincts.	1. You can listen to your tummy or the voice inside when something feels "icky" or wrong. 2. You can tell Mommy/Daddy if you have that icky feeling, even after it's happened.	1. If you have an "icky" or uncomfortable feeling, say no or leave. 2. You don't have to be polite to people who make you feel uncomfortable.	1. If something feels wrong, listen to that feeling. 2. You can tell if a person is trying to trick you by what he or she wants you to do.
If you are lost:	1. Look for a mommy. (A mommy is someone who is with kids.)	1. Prefer to look for a mommy but learn to recognize other	1. Have a pre-planned safety strategy— where to go if you

Teaching Points	3–5-Year-Olds	6–11-Year-Olds	12–17-Year-Olds
	2. Know your name, address, and phone number.	"helping" people if needed. 2. Be able to recognize store clerks, police officers, and security guards. 3. Don't wander around looking for your parent. Get help!	are lost, whom to call, etc. 2. Get help by calling a trusted adult—don't hitch-hike, take rides from strangers, or walk around an unknown area.
There are grown-ups who can help.	Always tell a grown-up if you feel scared or uncomfortable!	Keep telling grown-ups until you get the help you need.	If you don't feel comfortable talking to a parent, other trusted adults can help you. If you're a teen, you should know whom to go to for help—whatever the situation.
The one person you can always tell:	Always tell a teacher.	Always tell a teacher.	Always tell a teacher
Venturing out:	Check in and report in—tell your mommy when you're finished doing one thing and starting another thing.	Only go someplace with a trusted adult and ask permission of your mom or dad first.	Always let someone know where you are going and when you will return.
Communicate with your children by talking, listening, and observing.	Listen to what your kids say.	1. Allow for open communication. 2. Be interested and attentive, and encourage conversations. 3. Take seriously the information that your children give you.	1. Listen to what your child tells you—and recognize what is being omitted. 2. Make sure your child knows that you will believe him or her. 3. Don't judge or punish your child for openly dis-closing something that may frighten you.

QUESTION 18: IS IT OK TO TELL MY CHILDREN NEWS STORIES ABOUT SEXUALLY ASSAULTED CHILDREN?

Media sensationalism is a hotly contested issue. Most people accept that the media are a necessary source of information, but they bring with it spin, hysteria, or hype. The biggest problem, in my opinion, is that only newsworthy stories are discussed. The real, typical cases and those that happen every day are not always those that make the headlines. The dramatic ones slant our sense of real danger.

Perhaps the biggest upside to breaking stories on child sexual assault is that they remind parents and caretakers that child safety and sexual assault always need to be top of mind. We are all vulnerable, regardless of race, color, creed, socioeconomic status, and so on, when it comes to sexual assault. The biggest downside is the impression that "stranger danger" is the real concern. Cases that make the news are the abductions by strangers, the Internet crimes, the innocent children stolen, raped, and murdered by "that animal." As the statistics and my experience verify, the media cases are really the exception and pale in comparison to real cases, where the perpetrators are the people that parents and kids know, love, and trust.

How much information you want to share with your children is like any other judgment call. Some factors to consider include:

- How old is my child?
- How sensitive is my child? How easily frightened, worried, or stressed is he or she?
- What is the likelihood that my child is going to hear about the news story from other sources and thus be influenced by wrong information?
- Has the story been resolved, or is the offender still on the loose?
- How close is the case, geographically and personally, to our family's situation?
- How has my child reacted to other personal safety lessons?

The real issue is not actually watching the story—it's the opportunity for parents to use it to convey a lesson. If you, as a parent, decide that it is OK for a child to know what's really going on, then you must be prepared to hold a well-planned follow-up discussion to elaborate on the news story, answer questions, and see what messages the child has gotten.

News articles offer us an excellent opportunity to explain bad behavior and its consequences to our children. You should ask your children what they know about a particular news story, then use the facts to show which types of conduct are inappropriate. After the conversation, children should be asked what they learned so you can determine how well they understood the issues discussed. You might want to be prepared to answer questions that will arise after your discussion.

Besides talking to children about sexual abuse cases in the news, we need to teach our children a very important concept: that their body is their own, that nobody can touch them without their permission. We need to emphasize that no means no and that anybody who refuses to respect that should be considered dangerous and reported to the police. Finally, as parents, we need to let our children know that they can come to us at any time, without any fear or embarrassment. If they have been touched inappropriately, they need to know that it is never their fault.

You can determine how much information is enough, and how much is too much, by considering these factors:

1. What is the story?
2. How close to home is it?
3. Is there a message you must give to your child on this specific case?

Once you've made your decision, be comfortable with it. In this news-drenched society, kids pick up all kinds of information, so the better informed you are, the more you can protect and inform your child about possible threats to his or her security.

QUESTION 19: ARE INTERNET PREDATORS DIFFERENT FROM OTHER PREDATORS? WHY ARE THEY SO SUCCESSFUL?

Internet predators use the same techniques of grooming to gain access to children. The difference is inherent to the Internet itself.

Their targets sit in front of a computer screen and not outside in the open, usually in a private place like a bedroom or study. Children are increasingly using the Internet as a haven to share feelings, discuss taboo subjects, and make friends with people they have never met before. Internet predators are aware of the desires and insecurities of children and prey on them to satisfy their own warped fantasies.

It is usually harder to groom a child in person because of the presence of adults. Also, because most children cannot yet drive, predators are unable to lure them to an area where their criminal behavior can remain private. Predators can easily be identified in person—they have a recognizable face and voice that people can remember. On the Internet, predators can remain anonymous, using pseudonyms or screen names to hide their true identities. They can also manipulate their intended targets more successfully because they can choose what they want to say more carefully. A predator may give clues to indicate his ulterior motives when he starts talking about things that makes him nervous, such as sex.

Online predators provide something that parents tend not to give their kids enough—their undivided attention. Predators are patient when they communicate with their online targets. They shower the child with compliments, show intense interest in their potential victim's life, and are unconditional in their support of the child. Predators offer exactly what every child and teenager needs at the most confusing time of their life—someone who listens compassionately and attentively without passing judgment. Internet predators educate themselves about every aspect of children's likes and dislikes, including the latest trends and lingo. Unlike busy parents, they show their interest by staying completely focused on the child.

There are many types of Internet predators—ones who go into a chat room to fulfill their sexual desires, ones who actually travel long distances to groom a child met online (these predators are very persistent and skilled at what they do), and ones who chat with a child only to obtain the child's photo so they can satisfy their sexual fantasies. Children will often go into chat rooms or on social Web sites because they are bored. Unfortunately, they are often not educated enough about the dangers of connecting with strangers online. A child may give out personal information out of appreciation for the adult having listened to or "understood" him or her—qualities that the child's parent may lack.

Internet predators tend to seek out children who are vulnerable; therefore, they will search chat rooms until they can befriend a child who feels lonely, insecure, or depressed. Because children are curious, they want to explore subjects, such as sex, that they otherwise would not talk about with their parents. Even when children intend to publish their personal information so that only their peers can see it, predators can have access to that same information. Because of these dangers, parents have a responsibility to teach their children about the dangers of the Internet and make sure they are not publishing personal information accessible to anybody.

Parents should also be aware of behavior that indicates a child is hiding something, such as responding aggressively to questions about whom they're talking with online, gifts that they have received from someone unknown to the parents, or phone calls to your child from previously unfamiliar area codes or phone numbers.

The biggest benefit of the Internet is the access to so many different people in one place at one time. Kids see social-networking websites, such as MySpace, Facebook, Second Life, and YouTube, as places where they can express themselves, experiment, meet others, vent, and do all the things that kids do in the privacy of their own home.

The Internet is a wonderful source for predators because it allows them to study their prey. From one social-networking page, the predator can find out a child's name, his or her friends' names, where they go to school, whether the child's parents are married or divorced, what the child looks like, his or her hobbies, and such. Then, predators do exactly what we as parents don't do enough of—spend time talking and listening to that child.

While kids may have been told not to talk to strangers on the Internet, once a conversation begins, it may be very difficult to end, which is exactly what the predator hopes for. After earning the victim's initial trust, the predator will disclose that—surprise!—"I'm not as old as I said I was." In fact, the child will learn that his or her new Internet buddy is actually older than previously believed. Despite the lie, the victim is still likely to feel flattered that an older, more sophisticated person is eager to keep the contact going.

I train children to simply not respond and immediately delete any unknown person who pops up. If a child deletes a predator, the predator will simply move on. It's almost like the deterrent effect of the Club on a car's steering wheel. If a thief sees a car with the Club, he simply moves to the next vehicle. It's just too much work to deal with that car. Kids need to learn to delete—no discussions, no return IM, nothing—just delete. Unfortunately, there is more than enough potential prey for the predator.

Another reason predators like the Internet is for some of the same reasons that children do: it is a place to experiment—a shy person can be tough, a young person can be old, a bookworm can be hip. All is fair game in the land of fantasy created by the Internet.

Just as abstinence is the only one hundred percent effective birth control method, children should be taught that refusing to respond to an unknown e-mail, text, or instant message is the only one hundred percent effective method for keeping predators away. If a child consistently refuses to respond to unknown correspondents under any circumstances, there will be nothing to fear from online predators. Remember, once your child clicks Delete, the perpetrator will simply move on to other potential prey in cyberspace.

QUESTION 20: WHAT SHOULD MY FAMILY'S RULES BE REGARDING OUR CHILDREN'S USE OF THE INTERNET?

The Internet's popularity has risen substantially over the last two decades. As a result, molesters are increasingly using the Internet to target children. In particular, chat rooms are popular services that allow molesters to access children quickly and easily. Many times, children's need for attention and curiosity adds to their attraction to child molesters, who seek just such targets.

Therefore, to protect children from unwanted advances by molesters, parents need to establish family rules regarding computer use. These rules should allow the child to enjoy the Internet while giving the parent the control needed to monitor their children's safety. The delicate balance between privacy and disclosure of a child's life is not easy. Children want to participate and engage in activities that are free from parental interference. Parents want only what is best for their child, which, of course, includes their safety. A relationship built on truth and respect will greatly help children appreciate their parents' rules on Internet usage.

First, parents must explain the dangers of the Internet. Then, several practical rules should be devised and enforced—including setting up the times when children may go online and for how long. For example, children can be limited to one hour of computer time a night after homework is completed. Second, parents should teach their children not to give out any personal information when they are online, including their address, telephone number, and name. Third, parents should find out what Web sites their children visit, then research these sites to see what they include and whether they ask users to supply any personal information. Parents can actually track which sites their children visit simply by looking at their Web site history included on the tools menu of any Web browser. Fourth, children must never give out their password to anyone, even people they know. Sharing passwords with other people endangers a family's and a child's privacy. Fifth, children should let their parents know whenever they download and install any software or programs on their computer. This is especially true for software from private sites. Web sites may lure children through fancy advertisements or interesting topics, only to infect the computer with viruses that threaten the family's privacy.

Kids need to know four key facts about the Internet:

1. Cyberspace is never private or secure.
2. Sexually explicit photos or crude/demeaning comments can come back to haunt you.
3. There are consequences for online behavior.
4. People are not always who they say they are.

The best rules are those created as part of a collaboration between parents and children. After discussing Internet safety, they should jointly agree on appropriate rules to protect the child—and the family. When children are part of the process, they feel they "own" it and are more likely to be accountable and responsible.

Here are some suggestions to get your family started on realistic rules for Internet activity:

1. If you come across anything uncomfortable, speak up at once.
2. Never agree to meet in person anyone you have met online.
3. Never put anything online that you wouldn't feel comfortable screaming in a mall, on the street, or in a classroom hallway.
4. Never respond to an unsolicited invitation to chat, message, and so forth.
5. Just because someone is a "friend of a friend" does *not* mean that you know this person or that the "friend's" family shares our rules and values.
6. Never download anything without consulting me first.

A Word of Caution

One thing you need to be very careful about is how you react if your child discloses that someone they don't know sent an unsolicited comment, request, or note. Many parents panic and cut off all Internet access, saying, "See? This is why you can't be online." A parent who reacts this way is punishing the child for doing exactly what we want them to do—tell us. Kids who tell us about unsolicited requests online should be given positive reinforcement for recognizing the situation, for not responding (hopefully that's what they did), and for telling a responsible adult. No matter our age, we will encounter unwanted and unsolicited messages. It's what we do with them that either puts us in harm's way or lets us remove the danger.

QUESTION 21: SHOULD I ALLOW MY CHILD ON SOCIAL-NETWORKING SITES LIKE MYSPACE, FACEBOOK, OR SECOND LIFE?

We have all heard the expression that it's the symptom, not the disease. Many parents are quick to conclude that if the Internet is the problem, perhaps we should limit or forbid use of any sites that concern us. And since all parents were children once, we should remember just how well prohibition goes over. While I cannot dictate the rules of your home, I can offer reasons why you should allow responsible social networking on the sites you know and trust.

When evaluating social-networking sites, consider your child's age and level of development. Before you decide whether you will allow online activity, you should draw an offline parallel. Since MySpace and Facebook are, in some ways, similar to the soda shops of the fifties, the school dance of the sixties, the drive-ins of the seventies, and the malls of the eighties, think what would be acceptable for your children in those circumstances. Things that would not be OK in the real world should similarly be disallowed in the cyberworld.

One of the biggest mistakes I see parents making is prohibiting something they know nothing about. Before allowing your child to explore social-networking and similar Web sites, you as the parent should set up your own page on Facebook, MySpace, and the like—know how it works, learn the lingo, and log on regularly for changes and updates. Once you, as the parent, know what's going on, you will have a better sense of what to be concerned about and whether your child can use those sites. Invite your children to create a page with you. See how they approach designing their page. From that, you can engage in amiable conversation while getting a sense of just how computer savvy they are. You may even learn a few things!

Once your page and your child's page is set up, ask to be added as a buddy or friend on his or her page. This will give you the ability to access your kid's page and see what changes are made and when. Facebook and MySpace pages are a huge, untapped source of information for parents. If you want to know who is cool, who is having a party, who is dating whom, all you have to do is read the information on the kids' pages. You will learn more than you would from any conversation.

Like every other issue I have discussed, it is incumbent on you, the parent, to spot check your children. Send an anonymous friend or buddy request from a different (fake) profile and see how they respond. If they ignore you, delete you, or say no, then give yourself a big high five. If they engage in conversation, send you a message, or accept you as a friend, then tighten the rules regarding the Internet specifically and computer use in general, just as you would in any other situation when your child disobeys your wishes.

QUESTION 22: SHOULD I HACK INTO MY KIDS' COMPUTERS AND MONITOR THEIR WEB SITE USAGE?

Hacking into a child's computer is a sensitive issue for both the parent and child. No one likes the idea of spying, invading space, or destroying privacy. However, to simply let kids into the wild, wild west of the World Wide Web without so much as spot checking is simply foolish. In an age when the Internet has become the predominant form of communication, parents have a right to be concerned about what their children watch and whom they communicate with online. The goal of searching should not be to spy or to invade privacy but rather to gain intelligence, recognize potential problems, and stay in tune. It used to be that all parents had to do to get an idea of what their kids were up to was to listen, eavesdrop on some conversations, and be alert. Kids no longer beg for their own phone in their room; they want cell phones, computers, and other ways to communicate. And while the modes of communication may have changed, parents need to know that what's going on in their kids' lives has not.

We all know that the Internet can be a useful tool—academically and socially—in helping your child's development and growth. By being allowed to chat with her friends, and by establishing social connections with peers, your child can improve her communication and relational skills. Balanced against these are the negatives. The Internet has become a scarier place, becoming the preferred means for sexual predators to prey on young and vulnerable children. It has also become the easiest way for children to access sexually explicit content, such as pornographic pictures and videos. Facing these concerns, parents believe they have a duty to monitor their children's activities because they want to protect their children's safety and moral values. At the same time, invading a child's privacy could sabotage an open and communicative relationship between the child and the parent.

So what is the answer? Like every other parenting issue, much depends on the following factors:

- Who your kid is
- What your family rules are
- What your instincts tell you

Parents are in the best position, both from an actual and intuitive stand, to have a feel for who their child is and what their child is up to. The best way to confirm your worries or to head concerns off at the pass is to take a look-see. Who are my kids' friends on Facebook? What information do they post for the public to see? How vulnerable are they? While your kids may give you one version, there is no substitute for seeing it for yourself.

I believe in a balanced approach to your child's safety. Parents should raise independent adults capable of making thought-out, reasoned, and good decisions. Since that is our goal, there is no better way to see how they are doing than by seeing them in action. So, yes, I think parents should see what their kids are up to, but what needs to be balanced is how often you look, what you look for, and what you do with that information.

A child will undoubtedly feel that his or her space is invaded if a parent continues to pop up online. Parents need to pay particular attention regarding what warrants a reaction, a comment, or a discussion. The worst thing that could happen is that a parent blows his or her own cover, only for the child to create another page, screen name, and such, which the parent will never find.

If the point of good parenting is to develop a trusting and loving relationship between parent and child, then parents must ensure that they do not overstep their bounds. Therefore, invading a child's privacy should be saved only for those situations when obvious signs indicate that a child has been engaging in unlawful or unsafe activities or as periodic spot checks. If a parent thinks he or she is not skilled in identifying signs or, quite simply, does not have the time to observe them, some practical tips can minimize a child's exposure to dangerous content or people on the Internet:

1. *Put your computer in the living room.* This reduces your child's propensity to visit Web sites he or she otherwise would not have visited, since all eyes can see what your child does on the computer.
2. *Restrict Internet usage.* To develop a more trusting relationship, you can increase the amount of time your child may use the Internet if the child has obeyed previously set time limits.
3. *Talk gently about the dangers of the Internet.* That means you should listen to any objections or questions your child may have. Remember, children will respect you only if you respect them first.
4. *Be supportive.* Let your children know that you support their privacy and that you understand their wanting to become more independent. Remind them that they are responsible for their actions. By acknowledging your children's desire for independence, and communicating that you trust them in making their own decisions, you are developing a more trusting relationship with your children, which may encourage them to come forward with future troubles, both online and offline.
5. *Be honest.* Not many values are more important in children's relationships with their parents than honesty. If you snooped in the past, or plan on periodically checking your child's Internet activities, be honest with your child about your intentions. By creating an open dialogue regarding what you have done or may continue doing, you develop a line of communication that says, "Yes, I am doing these things, but do you understand why, or do you have any concerns?" If your child responds negatively, listen before judging. By understanding your child's concerns, you can better evaluate the best method for ensuring your child's safety, while at the same time strengthening your relationship.

QUESTION 23: WHAT FACTORS MAKE SOMEONE MORE LIKELY TO SEXUALLY ABUSE A CHILD?

No single factor can guarantee whether a perpetrator will attempt to sexually abuse a victim, but several factors can combine to increase the odds of abuse.

Listed below are some factors to consider when evaluating the potential risk level:

- *History of sexually abusive behavior:* If someone has previously acted in a sexually abusive manner, it's a strong indicator for future abuse because the person has acted on an *unnatural interest* in children and he or she has previously been aroused by a child.
- *Access:* This is someone who is often around the house, the school, the church, and other places and can spend time with the child. Child sexual abusers carefully place themselves in children's environments so they can seek out the perfect victim.
- *Isolation:* This involves someone who can isolate the child from others, either physically or mentally, by knowing the weaknesses in a child. For example, a perpetrator who knows a child's history of problems, like lying, drug/alcohol abuse, or developmental disabilities such as mental retardation or mental illness, can use these weaknesses to gain entry.
- *Parents' ability to protect:* A predator will assess the parents' ability to protect their child. Adults who are already under the predator's control and have shown they cannot even protect themselves are the least likely to protect their child.

The classic example of this is the domestic violence victim. An abuser knows he can sexually abuse his daughter because when he physically beats her mother, she does nothing to protect herself. If she can't protect herself how can she protect her child?

Besides helping to reduce the risk to children, these factors can help evaluate how genuine a child's disclosure might be when revealing a sexual assault. The best way to reduce risk is to foster these qualities in your children:

- a strong sense of self-worth and self-esteem
- confidence
- the ability to recognize a situation that is odd, threatening, or downright dangerous

Child molesters like to target vulnerable and needy children, specifically children in dysfunctional families. Usually, these children seek someone who can provide the love and security missing at home. With these victims, molesters are more confident that their manipulative advances will not be initially seen as abnormal or deviant.

Molesters are very good manipulators, and their goals often involve lowering a child's inhibitions to make him or her more receptive to perverse acts. Molesters will often invite a child to look at pornography or will make it available. Another example—more prevalent in older children—may involve offering alcohol and drugs to get the child to view the molester as a cool person. Molesters will often use charm and money to develop trust with their intended victims.

Oftentimes, molesters target victims in areas where most children and teenagers hang out, such as schools, arcades, parks, malls, and movie theaters. Other times, molesters target their own children or step-children. As a result, their acts usually occur at home.

Once a molester has started abusing the child, he will take steps to make sure that she will not tell anyone else so that the abuse can continue without the fear of being caught. Some examples of techniques molesters use include:

- promising gifts to the victim
- explaining that the touching was accidental
- commenting on how lonely the child will be without the relationship

These ploys are aimed at creating feelings of helplessness and self-blame that the molester hopes will work in his favor if he is ever caught.

QUESTION 24: WHAT SHOULD I DO ABOUT SLEEPOVERS?

There are actually two parts—one, should I let other kids sleep at my house?; two, should I let my kids sleep at someone else's place? The answer depends largely on your own upbringing and personal experiences. Whenever I ask a group of parents what they think the rule should be regarding sleepovers, I see some very smart, worldly, and loving parents who say "No way!" while across the aisle are parents who are equally smart, worldly, and loving who say, "Of course!" What to do?

I, personally, remember sleepovers as wonderful childhood experiences where I got to spend night time and bedtime with my closest friends. I became a member of a second family and enjoyed the different rules and landscape. I also enjoyed having friends see my house and how things were with my folks. So I come from the perspective that sleepovers can be wonderful, memorable experiences. But, as a prosecutor, I also know all the dangers. Yes, I have seen bad things happen at sleepovers; yes, I have had cases where someone's father touched another child at a sleepover.

But was the sleepover the culprit? In my mind, no, the culprit was the person, and the sleepover was the access. The perpetrator could easily access the same child whether or not he or she had slept over As with other decisions, with sleepovers, parents should evaluate whose house is a safe place for their children to play. The more you know about the host family, and the more you know about yourself, the more likely you will be to make a decision that is good for you and your children.

Some questions that will lead you to the best answer are:

- At whose house will the sleepover be held?
- Do you know all the people who live or stay at the house?
- What do you feel about each person individually at the house?
- Is there anyone there who makes you feel uncomfortable?
- How long have you known the parents or caretakers?
- Are the parents going to be home?
- Is the parent supervising single?
- If there will be a nanny or a babysitter, who is it?
- Is your child going to bathe there?
- If so, who does the bathing?
- Are any other children going to spend the night?
- What activities are planned?
- Is the plan to stay in the whole night?
- Does your child know that she can call you anytime, even in the middle of the night, if she feels uncomfortable?
- Can you communicate the previous question comfortably with the other parent?
- Where will you be during the sleepover?
- Do you feel that your child can make good decisions?
- How have you done in educating your child about body safety and good touch/bad touch?

QUESTION 25: CAN SCHOOLS HIRE A TEACHER WHO HAS BEEN ACCUSED OF SEX ACTS WITH CHILDREN?

Every day, parents send children to school with the expectation that they will be safe, will learn, and are in the good hands of teachers. When we walk our children in, drop them off, and wave good-bye, we are essentially "blessing" the school, giving our children the message that we trust this place or we would not leave them there.

Parents instinctively know that they must pay a lot of attention in hiring nannies and babysitters, but they seem to forget to do a background check of their children's schools. Yes, parents spend a great deal of energy in choosing their kids' schools, but they focus on academic offerings, sports, and extracurricular activities. Questions that need to be asked include:

- What is the student-teacher ratio?
- Where does your pool of substitute teachers come from?
- What is your hiring process?
- Do you conduct background checks?
- Are substitute teachers put through the same vetting process as full-time teachers and faculty?
- What types of things would disqualify a candidate from working here?
- What is your policy about teachers/administrators with substance abuse histories?
- Are there policies addressing weapons, sexual abuse, child-on-child abuse, substance abuse, and violence?
- How do you screen the people who work with the students who are not teachers (e.g., specialists, volunteers, bus drivers, cafeteria workers)?
- Can I visit the school at any time?

Currently, there is no federal law to prevent a state from allowing a teacher accused of sexual assault to teach in another district or state. Although a child's safety should be the school's first priority, many districts choose not to report sexual abuses that may have occurred between a teacher and student because schools are afraid of wrongfully accusing a teacher for an act that has not yet been proven. The driving force behind this mentality is the fear of civil lawsuits by the accused and from other parents and the bad publicity that comes from such lawsuits no matter how the case turns out.

Another issue schools wrestle with is privacy. This may explain why some school administrators are reluctant to release the personnel file of a teacher previously accused of sexual misconduct.

Many school districts endanger students by allowing the accused teacher to resign or to retire from the district. By choosing not to deal with the problem, school districts are "passing the trash"—a phrase to describe a school district that allows a teacher accused of abuse to leave quietly—and irresponsibly permitting predators to teach in other districts where abuse may continue.

Ironically, many school districts may have an incentive to report suspected sexual abuse to other school districts and school officials who grant teacher licenses. There is an increasing number of lawsuits filed by alleged victims against any school district that fails to report suspected abuse. Therefore, as the number of civil lawsuits grows, so, hopefully, will the responsibility of school districts to disclose information about a teacher's past misconducts.

Fortunately, some states have made it easier for school districts to encourage reporting. For instance, in California and Michigan, state law forbids school districts from negotiating a teacher's resignation in exchange for silence of past allegations of abuse against a student. In a minority of states, the law requires people who know about the abuse to report it. For example, if teacher 1 knows that teacher 2 is abusing a child, teacher 1 must report to school officials, law enforcement, or the mandated department for protection of children services. While not adopted in all states, this is a step in the right direction.

Schools that make children's safety their number-one priority are proactive in taking steps to avoid sexual exploitation. Besides reporting unseemly conduct, schools need to actually toe the ethical line, always cognizant of the impression they make in day-to-day choices. With that in mind, teachers should not:

- be allowed to be alone with children in the classroom
- arrange to meet students outside school other than for parent conferences
- transport students to events, field trips, and elsewhere
- entertain students in their own homes

My guess is that with more media focusing on sexual abuse at school, both student-on-student as well at teacher-on-student, we are likely to see schools implementing more guidelines to ensure the protection of children.

QUESTION 26: DO SCHOOLS DO BACKGROUND CHECKS ON EMPLOYEES SUCH AS TEACHERS, STAFF, AND ADMINISTRATORS?

With growing concerns about child sexual assault, people often question what background checks—if any—are made before hiring a teacher, staff member, or school administrator.

Like many issues we have seen, even the term *background checks* is subject to multiple meanings. When used in the school setting, a background check is the process by which the teacher must get fingerprinted by the school's local law enforcement agency. The fingerprinting process reveals any criminal histories that a school or school district can evaluate.

The criminal background check is a start but should by no means be the end. Criminal history checks are not foolproof, nor do they give a complete picture of a person. For example, basic criminal background checks often do not catch so-called mobile molesters—those who move on to new districts, sometimes in other states, leaving behind a trail of victims. These people are not caught because they leave an area before an investigation can even be done; thus, they never acquire a criminal history. The problem of mobile molesters also needs to be addressed, rather than quietly ignored, at schools that hire a teacher and discover that he or she acted inappropriately or even criminally.

Background checks should not be limited to the staff member's initial hiring. There must be ongoing due diligence and continued (random) checking, as criminal histories are constantly updated. Schools should be privy to the most current information. If a teacher gets a new job prior to an official criminal investigation, then a criminal history may appear to be clean when in fact it is not.

Stringent background checks on prospective employees should include contacting previous employers, specifically regarding any terminations or investigations brought against the applicant. Schools should also be required to readily disclose such personnel matters to other schools. Too often, schools do not communicate with other schools and worry only about the health and safety of its own campus. Currently, the only communication between schools is in public schools where district offices are involved. There is no official coordination between private schools. To assist schools' communication in protecting children, there should be a national requirement that all districts report all instances of termination caused by sexual exploitation.

Prior to making a job offer, school personnel should read all the information from the current employer and confirm its accuracy. To make background screens even more effective, schools should check for gaps in employment, ask why an applicant moved between schools or districts, contact school personnel in previous sites beyond those listed as references, ask direct questions, and search driving-under-the-influence offenses. All social security numbers of new hires should be verified. Finally, every offer of employment should include a probationary period.

While screening will not identify all potential predators, it does signal seriousness on the part of the school, the district, and the state.

QUESTION 27: SHOULD I LET MY CHILD PLAY OUTSIDE IN THE NEIGHBORHOOD?

Studies show that children spend less time playing outside than their parents did when they were young. No wonder so many children today are obese! By staying indoors, children are not getting the physical exercise they need to prevent obesity and other health risks—unless you consider typing on the computer a good finger exercise.

Indoor activities include watching television, spending hours on the Internet, and playing video games. Some parents argue that playing outdoors is no longer safe and that the only alternative is to let children stay indoors. However, parents do not realize that computer use without proper supervision can be just as dangerous. That's why I recommend that children should be allowed to play outdoors, but only with proper supervision.

Playing outdoors can do wonders for our kids, improving their social, emotional, and physical development. Children get the chance to interact with others around their age, which can help strengthen their communication and social skills. When a kid is locked up in a house with just his or her computer and video games, very little human interaction occurs. Chatting online is not the same as talking in person because the spoken word adds more context to a description of an event or a reaction to a situation. In addition, letting children choose whether they want to play with the monkey bars, for example, may bring out emotions they have never experienced, such as fear and curiosity. In a way, allowing children to experience new things is similar to making them feel more independent. While exposing your child to the emotions of pain, fear, and frustration may seem cold and calculating, without these experiences, your child will have more difficulty discovering his or her own feelings in the future.

Finally, letting your child play outdoors will help combat the threat of obesity and poor eating habits. You know that exercise is good for you, so the next time you see your child speeding through the playground thinking he's the world's greatest sprinter, encourage him that he could someday be a gold medalist if he keeps working at it. Parents can encourage their younger children to become physically active by taking them to a park or taking a mini-vacation to an outdoor event, such as camping or hiking. That way, they can supervise their child's safety while encouraging an active lifestyle. As children grow older, or when parents feel that they have sufficiently matured, they can give their children more freedom and allow them to play outdoors without adult supervision.

First, set up ground rules. Tell your children that they cannot stay past a certain time or that they cannot go farther than a certain part of the park or playground. If your children have been left unsupervised, you should always know who will be playing with them. It is also a good idea to exchange text or phone messages with other kids' parents to see how your own child is behaving. Moreover, let your children know that if they ever feel uncomfortable with another person, for whatever reason, they should come home immediately, or if they can't, have them call you to pick them up.

All children should possess certain safety skills. They should:

- Be in tune to their instincts—recognize when something feels wrong, a person is acting improperly, or a situation warrants leaving it.
- Make it a ritual to check in, physically when out on the streets and by phone when away from home.
- Know that it is always OK to *leave, run,* and *say no.*
- Know whom to go to for help and how to identify helpful people: moms are the best bet.

QUESTION 28: HOW CAN I FIND OUT IF REGISTERED SEX OFFENDERS LIVE NEAR ME?

Simply go to your local law enforcement office. By law, states are required to disclose the names and addresses of all registered sex offenders living in the state.

In many states, you can access a list of them online, and some states even include a picture of the sex offender, as well as his criminal record relating to any sexual acts. Some communities have meetings to notify residents of sexual offenders in their area; others notify residents by mail. Once notified, parents should follow some practical tips to ease their concerns.

Do not panic. Having a sexual offender living in your area should not stop you from doing what you do daily; it should also not stop your kids from following their daily routine. By not panicking or feeling upset, you can better prepare yourself to take the necessary steps to protect your children without the cloud of suspicion hovering over every individual you encounter. You're also empowered by not allowing the presence of an offender to change the way you live.

Follow up on notifications. When parents are notified of an offender living in the neighborhood, either by mail, in person, or at meetings, they can follow up on the offender's background, usually via his parole officer. By getting the name and phone number of the parole officer assigned to the offender, parents can ask what, if any, changes the offender made while in jail and how committed the offender really is to changing his behavior. In addition, having more information about a sex offender's background can tell parents what locations he or she likes to frequent and his or her habits.

Know if the offender is restricted. After speaking with the offender's parole officer, you may find out what restrictions the offender may be placed under, such as keeping a specific distance from schools or locations where kids congregate or being required to constantly wear a GPS monitor. By knowing these restrictions, you will know what to report if the offender ever violates any of them.

Show your support. Although not for everybody, you may show your support for the convicted offender by going with another neighbor or friend to welcome him to the neighborhood. This approach is advocated by those who believe that people can change when surrounded by the right influences. It is intended to help the offender feel accepted—with reservations—and not looked upon as a monster because of his previous acts. If this approach is decided upon, it should be reinforced by a background check through the offender's parole or probation officer. You want to know that the person is truly sorry for his crime and that he is genuinely intent on turning his life around. This is not necessarily a step I personally would take, but perhaps a relationship with a registrant will squelch the fears of the unknown and remove some of the mystery behind who the registrant is.

QUESTION 29: AS A SINGLE MOM, WHAT SHOULD I DO IF I LEARN THAT THE MAN I'M DATING IS A SEX OFFENDER?

If you're dating a sexual offender, you need to keep your children as far away from him as possible until you can gather more specific information about his previous crimes. Some things to consider are how you received information, how long ago the crime was committed, and what the nature of the crime was.

Many registered sex offenders have restrictions that prevent them from being near schools, public parks, and places where youth usually gather. However, most laws do not prevent sexual offenders from being around children in general.

As a parent, the most important thing is to look out for your child's health and safety. Allowing a convicted sex offender to be a part of your life may endanger your child. Therefore, if you find out that a sex offender has either violated his parole or any restrictions placed on him, you need to contact your local law enforcement. Obviously, anyone willing to violate the rules placed upon him cannot be trustworthy.

There is a distinction, however, between a child sex offender and a sex offender in general. While it does not lessen the seriousness of the offender's act, it does affect who the offender's next victim would most likely be. A sex offender who has committed a crime against an adult will more likely harm an adult than a child. The opposite is true for a child sex offender.

If as a parent you decide to continue dating a sex offender, you should notify your ex-husband, who has a right to know the possible dangers his child may be exposed to. While there is room in all of us to believe that people can change, a mother's first concern should be for her child and her own safety. Unless the crime was committed many years ago and the offender has shown significant improvement through counseling, along with a convincing history of doing good deeds, a single mother should walk away from a potential powder keg of a relationship for the sake of her child.

QUESTION 30: AS A DIVORCED DAD, IS IT OK IF I BATHE MY PRESCHOOL DAUGHTER?

A father's involvement in the care of young children is to be truly valued for all the positive influences it brings. At the same time, protecting a child from inappropriate sexual behavior is obviously essential.

Bathing a child is a responsibility that parents have, and it's sad that this is a question I am repeatedly asked. But I think the real question that people are asking is "Am I going to be arrested for committing a crime when I am bathing my child?"

Unfortunately, particularly in divorce/custody situations, parents (particularly fathers) have to be concerned about whether they can take on a necessary parenting role like bathing their own children. In my opinion, this question is so often asked because of how messy divorces can be and how the criminal justice system can often be misused to affect a divorce or custody case.

I would like to remind parents that everybody's best interest should be focused on the child. It is *not* in the best interest of a child for one parent to quiz, manipulate, suggest, or imply inappropriateness where it does not exist. A vindictive parent who turns an innocent parenting duty into a sexual molestation case when it doesn't exist is not only harming her own child but also tainting the genuine sexual assault investigations out there.

With this in mind, my immediate response is yes, fathers should bathe their daughters if they are young enough to need bathing assistance. A father, whether divorced, married, single, or whatever, should be able to comfortably perform the duties of getting a child bathed, dressed, and off to bed or out to school.

However, circumstances where a father (or anyone, for that matter) should not be bathing a child—any child—include if:

- he has been convicted of any child sexual assault crimes
- he knows he has an unnatural interest in children even if it never has been acted out on, reported, or amounted to a crime
- *he* feels uncomfortable bathing the child
- the child feels uncomfortable

Bathing a child is a parental responsibility, not a time of sexual gratification for either the child or the parent. For someone to be charged with a lewd act when bathing a child, under most state laws, there must be a desire to appeal to the sexual interest of either the child or the perpetrator. The legal term is having *sexual intent*. While sexual intent is usually obvious from the act itself, merely touching the child's private parts with a washcloth would not be a lewd and lascivious act. That is not to say that that touching with a washcloth cannot initiate other acts that demonstrate sexual intent. Sexual intent can be shown if the bathing is coupled with inappropriate behavior, such as if the father is aroused, makes sexual comments, penetrates the child manually while bathing, or masturbates while bathing—these acts are all clearly sexual and clearly intended!

When dealing with bathing, the same lessons about body safety/privacy should apply. Children who are uncomfortable should know that they can say no—even in situations that involve their own parents doing what may seem like mundane activities, like bathing, but that cover up more sexual purposes.

QUESTION 31: HOW SHOULD I SCREEN A BABYSITTER OR NANNY?

Finding a childcare provider such as a babysitter or nanny can be challenging. I often tell parents that the most difficult part of being a parent is finding people they can trust to help take care of their children. Besides my own concerns as a parent, I need to find someone my child will like and trust. At some point, you will need to rely on other people to assist with child care.

Some of us are fortunate enough to have parents or grandparents who can help. But with lifespans increasing and our society's elders staying active, finding a grandparent who's available can be a challenge.

Modern society has made childcare more challenging, too, as few people stay in one place for very long. People move for school, jobs, relationships, and other reasons. Society's increasing mobility has led to short relationships and less accountability among people in general and among caretakers in particular.

You should take these steps when hiring a babysitter, a nanny, or other caretaker:

1. Decide what type of candidate you are seeking. Be brutally honest with yourself: what is your ideal—qualifications, age, gender, hours needed, priorities, etc.
2. Make a recruiting plan. Are you going to seek word-of-mouth referrals only or also try advertisements and agencies?

3. Write out a job description, including your expectations and what the caretaker can expect from you.

4. Note your initial responses to your search, including phone manner, e-mail correspondences, and anything that strikes you as bizarre or particularly good.

5. Schedule the first interview without the child present and make sure candidates bring the following documents:

- a driver's license (or other government-issued photo identification)
- a social security card/work permission
- a printout of the driving record (if your position requires driving)
- proof of auto insurance
- a resume
- the names and numbers of at least three references

6. Do a preliminary background check if you like the candidate.
7. Schedule a second interview with the child and the other parent.
8. Do a complete background check.

Recruiting

When the time comes to hire a nanny and/or babysitter, parents should make a candidate-recruiting plan. Recruiting requires research, both into the type of help you realistically need and an awareness of the going rates for that help. Who is your ideal? Are you looking for Mary Poppins, Fran from *The Nanny*, or someone who can cook and clean? To help determine what kind of assistant you need, you must consider the age of your children, the hours of help required, and your family's priorities. While having one person who can do it all seems ideal, it is unrealistic for one person to watch a couple of toddlers and cook and clean.

Once you have an ideal profile in mind, you need to know where to look. If you're looking for a more professional nanny or sitter, your best bet may be an agency. If you just need short-term help, perhaps a mature, reliable teenager will do the trick.

Sources within the community, such as the local law enforcement office, a social service agency, or even schools may help parents in their search for lists of recommended childcare providers. If you are part of a religious community, your church or the YMCA or YMHA is another good way to find reliable and trustworthy people. Finally, asking coworkers and friends for references can help identify care providers with previous experience with whom you can, with some confidence, feel safe.

Some words of wisdom: while teenagers are popular choices as babysitters, many may lack the experience or true desire to work with children. They may not be mature enough to make sound decisions, especially when it comes to inviting their friends over.

I am often asked about male babysitters or nannies. While I am not sexist, I do urge parents to keep the statistics in mind—most sexual assaults are perpetrated by males. Like everything else, whom you choose depends on their qualifications, experience, references, and your gut feeling.

Interview Process

Once you have found a childcare provider, make sure you interview the person thoroughly. Ask lots of questions that relate to his or her history dealing with kids, and observe, if possible, how well this person can interact with kids. The interview is the opportunity for the potential caretaker to talk and for you to listen. Following is a list of suggested questions to include in your interview. But remember that any question that isn't fully answered should be followed with more questions.

General Questions

- Why do you want to be a nanny/babysitter?
- How long have you been in childcare?
- Do you see yourself being a lifelong nanny or babysitter? If not, what are your goals?
- Do you have children/younger siblings?
- How would you describe your temperament and personality?
- Have you ever bathed a child?
- How do you feel bathing a child?
- What is your philosophy about discipline?
- What do you think your strengths are?
- What do you think your weaknesses are?
- Have you ever been in an emergency situation while babysitting? Tell me about it.

- How do you deal with a child or situation that frustrates you?
- What will you do if a child won't go to sleep?
- How do you deal with tantrums?
- Do you still nanny or babysit for any of your former employers?
- Why did you leave your last job?
- What do you think your former employers would say about you? Your strengths? Your weaknesses?
- I am planning on doing a background check on you. Is there anything you would be concerned about me finding?
- What questions do you have for me?

If the Nanny/Sitter Will Be Driving

- Are you comfortable driving children in the car?
- May I see your driver's license?
- How many years have you been driving?
- Do you have any marks against your driving record (speeding or accidents)?

If Newborns Are Involved

- Are you comfortable sitting for newborns?
- Can you change a diaper?
- Do you know infant CPR?
- Can you properly pick up and carry a newborn?
- Do you know about SIDS and how to prevent it?
- Can you prepare and heat formula correctly?
- Are you familiar with Shaken Baby Syndrome?
- Do you know the proper size for baby chewable vitamins?
- Do you know how to prevent or address choking?
- What are the signs that a room is childproofed?

Due Diligence

To further ensure the effectiveness and quality of the childcare provider, don't forget to cross-check every reference. When calling these references, ask about how well the children were cared for. After deciding on a provider, explain the family rules, such as how long children are allowed to stay up, how much time they can spend on the computer, and what types of food they can eat. You should also provide an emergency plan, including the phone numbers of the family doctor, law enforcement, and fire department. Always write down all the provider's information, including his or her phone number, address, and license plate number.

If you are looking for childcare providers who will work outside your home, such as from their home or a daycare facility, be sure you do background checks. Parents should also ask who accompanies their young children when they need to go to the bathroom. It is important that parents make sure that the bathrooms are open and not in some isolated, private part of the facility.

Screening babysitters is an absolute must, and it begins from the very first contact, whether by e-mail or by phone. From the second you receive a response to your advertisement, you should be filing away information about the candidate.

Your responsibility does not end once you have hired someone. Some ongoing responsibilities include the following:

1. Have a backup plan with babysitters on call whose backgrounds have been cleared and who know your home. You should use your backup help regularly to be sure you always have a stand-by in an emergency. We are most vulnerable and therefore make our kids most vulnerable when we have no contingency plan, such as when the regular sitter gets sick, there's a family emergency, and so forth.
2. Check in regularly. Come in unannounced and be unpredictable. There is no better way to know what's going on than to arrive when least expected.
3. Have other people check in on the children to get a sense of what goes on when you're not around. Be prepared to hear things you don't want to, and have a plan if you learn something that you do not approve of.
4. Listen to your children and your instincts. If something bothers you, communicate with the nanny. If there is any hint of abuse, whether verified or not, get rid of the caretaker.

QUESTION 32: SHOULD I GET A "NANNY-CAM" OR OTHER SURVEILLANCE PRODUCT?

In the past, surveillance equipment was used only by the government and private investigators. But now more and more people are wanting the peace of mind associated with this type of specialized equipment. With the recent rise in television shows featuring hidden cameras capturing the disturbing violent activities of a childcare provider, parents are becoming more cautious about their children's safety. As technology grows, so has the number of nanny-cams that are easy for parents to install and disguise from prospective caretakers. Nanny-cams are hidden cameras placed inside homes to monitor the activities of another person, usually a nanny or a babysitter. Before deciding whether to purchase a nanny-cam, parents must first consider the legal and ethical issues involved.

In all fifty states, it is legal to install a hidden camera in your home. However, federal law makes it illegal for a person to place a hidden camera in a bathroom or dressing room. The general rule is that a person who is not the homeowner cannot be filmed in an area where he or she expects privacy. The courts have ruled that filming a person in a kitchen, living room, and child's bedroom are all considered legal. In a significant number of states, it is illegal to film or make anything related to an audio recording of a person's conversations without the person's consent. Parents who commit an illegal activity may be subject to civil and criminal prosecution.

Ethically, parents must decide whether to let prospective caretakers know that they will be monitored. One benefit is that it may actually deter a nanny from committing abuse if she knows she is being taped. And any nanny who objects to being monitored may not be someone you want to hire anyway.

Many nannies do not necessarily object to being taped, but they do object to being lied to or misled. However, disclosure can also arm the nanny, who may have knowledge of privacy laws, to commit abuses in areas where she knows she is protected, such as the bathroom or her own bedroom. Finally, if you do decide to tell a prospective childcare provider about your intent to use a nanny-cam, have both parties—you and the caretaker—sign an agreement that states what you will be doing, to remove yourself from any future liability or legal issues.

After considering both the legal and ethical issues involved, a parent must carefully choose what type of nanny-cam is best and where to put it. Technological advances have made it possible for nanny-cams to be disguised in the form of a teddy bear, pen, clock, or plant. Regardless of whether you have disclosed to the childcare provider that you are monitoring her, you need not reveal where you have placed the camera. Therefore, nanny-cams should be in obscure places, for instance, in a clock in a child's bedroom.

If you want to confirm any suspicions, forget about the nanny-cam and follow your instincts. Why wait to catch an offense to your child on tape? Then it's too late!

Nanny-cams can be an effective method to spot check what goes on in your home when you're not around. Besides capturing any images of sexual assault, they can also be used to protect your personal property, observe whether your child is being properly attended to, and ensure that no unwanted or unknown people are in the house.

There is really no downside to getting a nanny-cam, other than the false sense of security it creates. Remember, a nanny-cam does not prevent abuse, inappropriate behavior, or crime. Nor can it necessarily capture everything. It is only one tool to give you more information on what happens at home when you're not around. If you wish to use a nanny-cam, do remain vigilant about talking to your kids about personal and body safety, always observe signs of inappropriate behavior, and follow your instincts.

Some people equate nanny-cams with invasive spying and prefer not to use them. If that's how you feel, then you must be extravigilant when interviewing candidates, doing background checks, and finding other ways to monitor care-givers' behavior.

PART THREE

RECOGNIZING ABUSE

QUESTION 33: SHOULD I REPORT A SUSPECTED CHILD ABUSER TO THE POLICE OR DO I NEED TANGIBLE EVIDENCE?

If you ever suspect that any crime has been committed, whether it's child sexual abuse, child abuse, or anything else, always choose to let the police know what's going on. Police departments are responsible for investigating complaints and determining whether a crime has occurred.

One of the biggest problems in investigating possible child sexual abuse occurs when parents take on the role of investigator. Not only does this not help an investigation, but it can actually work against it. Talking to the suspect is one of the best tools that police officers have. But a suspect who believes that someone is onto him could flee the area before the police talk to him, spend time preparing lies to cover up the abuse, or, worse yet, become violent. Just as you would never fill your own cavity or do surgery on yourself, no one other than law enforcement, child protective services, or other investigative agencies should conduct an investigation.

I've heard about concerned parents who have called their lawyer to make a report or to inquire about the reporting process. Although some very good-hearted and well-intentioned lawyers are out there, a good lawyer should refer a parent to law enforcement or child protective services.

Here's the bottom line: If you have a suspicion, a concern, a question, or a worry about an individual, make a report to the police. It will be up to the investigators—not you—to decide what course of action to take.

QUESTION 34: WHAT ARE THE SIGNS THAT A CHILD HAS BEEN IMPROPERLY TOUCHED?

A victim of sexual abuse may experience any number of physical, emotional, or behavioral reactions. Of course, any of these responses can indicate that the child has been touched, or they can indicate some other traumatic occurrence or life change. Nonetheless, if coupled with the news that a child has been abused, these symptoms should be examined, since they are typical of child victims.

Perhaps the most common and easily overlooked sign of abuse occurs when a child has a *sudden change in behavior*. For example, a once outspoken child who suddenly becomes withdrawn or shy can indicate sexual abuse. A child who was previously comfortable wearing shorts and now wants to wear only bulky sweaters (even in summer) may be experiencing a need to cover up his or her body.

Other common symptoms include:

- *Greater, new, or age-inappropriate fears:* These can include fear of the dark, strangers, being alone, germs. While a parent may want to excuse a fear from the child's earlier years, a sudden regression should be explored. For example, a child who at fifteen is suddenly afraid of the dark or fears being alone may be reacting to an abusive situation.
- *Sexual acting out:* This can involve promiscuous behavior, touching others, excessive masturbating, inserting objects into genitals or rectum, reenacting sexual acts, or excessive conversations about sex. For example, a parent who learns that her four-year-old is sharing oral sex with another four-year-old child should ask herself, "Where did my child learn this behavior?"
- *Eating problems:* These can include changes in eating patterns, loss of appetite, and noticeable weight loss or gain.
- *Bedwetting/soiling:* Potty-trained children suddenly lose control of their bowels or urinate while asleep or even while awake.
- *Sleep difficulties:* There is a new reluctance or an inability to sleep or wake up and a new tendency toward nightmares and night terrors.
- *Avoidance of specific people, situations, or activities:* Suddenly, the child shuns activities that at one time were fun or routine, such as sports, showers, school, certain family activities. Perhaps out of nowhere, a child refuses to be with a specific person that he or she originally enjoyed being with.
- *Physical issues:* These can include headaches, vomiting, weight gain, loss of menstrual cycle.

These symptoms should be checked out if your child continually demonstrates one or more of them. If they accompany a disclosure of sexual abuse, recognize that they, along with the following list of emotional reactions, are normal and should be expected:

- Guilt
- Denial
- Fear
- Ambivalence
- Anger
- Depression
- Hurt
- Distrust
- Embarrassment
- Confusion
- Avoidance
- Powerlessness

These feelings can come up in a variety of ways and may be directed at any number of people involved in the legal system. Often a child victim will experience these emotions repeatedly. While some emotions may seem contradictory, a child is likely to feel simultaneous, competing emotions about different aspects of the abuse. For example, a child may feel ambivalent about the perpetrator but be angry at the parent for "letting" the abuse happen in the first place.

QUESTION 35: WHAT ARE THE POTENTIAL WARNING SIGNS OF TEACHER MISCONDUCT?

First, let me reiterate a theme that runs throughout this book: children are more endangered by people they know than by strangers. When it comes to abuse by educators, this is particularly shocking, as teachers have the trust of, and access to, many children and families.

Parents should be aware of any behavior, actions, or comments that seem inappropriate, and should explore these without delay. There may well be resistance, however, as educators, school districts, and even parents do not like to believe that teachers—individuals we charge with educating our children—

could abuse or exploit a child. Here are some potential warning signs that an educator may be sexually abusing or exploiting a child:

- Inappropriate comments and stories in class
- Singling out a student for preferential treatment
- Having particular students come to the classroom outside class time
- Repeatedly spending time in private places with students
- Buying students gifts
- Driving a student to and/or from school
- Flirtatious behavior
- Playful snapping of bra straps
- Comments about clothes, makeup, sex
- Writing notes or e-mails having nothing to do with class
- Calling a student on the phone
- Stopping by the student's home
- Trying to befriend a particular student's parents
- Brushing up or rubbing against a student
- Discussing sexual experiences
- Serving or showing a willingness to buy alcohol or drugs
- Showing pornographic or inappropriate material
- Taking the same children on outings or trips

The teacher has one other effective means of grooming at his fingertips that may not be available to other people—the opportunity to help troubled students with schoolwork, give extra credit, and even change a student's grades. Clearly, some signs are more obvious than others. After all, child molesters operate on a continuum of behavior that may start with a little extra attention then move to a violation of teacher-student boundaries and finally to molestation or other forms of abuse.

While all abuse is unforgivable, there is something particularly distressing about teachers who abuse their students. First of all, children rely on teachers as models of appropriate behavior in our society. By observing secrecy and controlling behavior, children become more open to becoming victims of other perpetrators because it seems like the norm.

QUESTION 36: WHAT ARE THE QUALITIES OF UNNATURAL SEXUAL BEHAVIOR?

A child's sexual behavior can be a significant indicator of whether he or she has been sexually abused. Age-inappropriate behavior is referred to as *unnatural sexual behavior*. For example, beginning to inquire about sex is appropriate for a teenager but probably not for a five- or six-year-old. Another strong indicator is the significant sexual knowledge a child of a specific age suddenly possesses.

Although curiosity is a natural characteristic of child development, some acts are considered so rare that they must be followed up by a parent or responsible guardian. These acts include a child:

- inserting objects into genitals or private parts
- making a proposition for sex
- intentionally grabbing a private part of another person
- using sexual words
- kissing or rubbing another person's private parts
- mimicking and echoing sexual noises
- asking to see sexually explicit content (pornography videos and magazines)
- acting out different sexual positions with clothes on
- having unusual knowledge of the sexual vocabulary
- wanting to know more about sex

To emphasize again, these acts are only signs that *may* indicate abuse but may also just be a part of the child's development. Parents know their children better than anyone and should be able to make intelligent assessments regarding the normalcy of a child's behavior.

Signs of sexual abuse are not always obvious. Parents need to be aware of abrupt behavior changes. For example, children with cuts or burn marks indicate something irregular that should be investigated. If the marks are self-inflicted, the child needs help. Another sign is a change in the child's eating habits. A formerly healthy child who becomes anorexic (not eating) or bulimic (eating then vomiting) indicates something serious. A little girl's decision to act older than she really is may be a response to abuse. For instance, a ten-year-old may inexplicably begin wearing high heels and short skirts when such attire is inappropriate for someone so young. By themselves, cuts and eating disorders may indicate other psychological issues in the child's life, but when coupled with the previously mentioned signs they strongly suggest sexual abuse.

Other indicators of abuse can be the child's emotional responses. For example, a child who adamantly refuses to visit another relative, parent, or friend of the parents may have been abused by that individual. Therefore, a disproportionate response to a person or a specific location (school, church, daycare center) may indicate cooperation with the abuser. Another response is a child's sensitivity to her environment. A young girl may cringe whenever someone walks past her or speaks to her, or she may constantly look over her shoulder to be sure she won't be accosted.

Parents should remember that while the above may be indicators of abuse, only further investigation and inquiry will determine whether there is actual abuse.

QUESTION 37: WHAT DO I DO IF I AM UNCOMFORTABLE WITH THE WAY SOMEONE ACTED, EVEN THOUGH HE NEVER TOUCHED MY CHILD OR SAID ANYTHING DIRECTLY SEXUAL?

If you feel uncomfortable about something—whether tangible or not—you are right. And whatever you do, don't spend a minute second-guessing yourself or rationalizing anybody's behavior. That uncomfortable feeling is telling you something, and you owe it to your child and yourself to listen to it, period. Regardless of whether abuse is actually occurring, something that makes you uncomfortable warrants investigation.

Our instincts help us survive. They are the part of our brains that react on autopilot and think for us. Since instincts do all the thinking work, why is it that people find reasons to push them aside? Instincts are not rational and not based on logic; while they may not give you exact answers, they are telling you something. When it comes to protecting children, particularly from sexual assault, parents and children must listen to their instincts. There is simply no downside to being overly cautious with people you or your children interact with. Your instincts will help guide you to who is OK and who is not.

I am constantly shocked by how often people doubt their own feelings, look for excuses to give people a second chance, and want to fight their gut feelings about someone. Why? Because they feel guilty about possibly hurting someone's feelings.

Kids need to develop and use their instincts to grow into self-sufficient adults. How can children do that if their role models suppress their own instincts when it is most important—for their children's protection?

What does all this instinct talk amount to? Very simply, if you are getting a weird vibe from someone, it's for a reason. When it comes to your kids, your job is not to explore the reason for the bad vibe but to make sure that person does not have access to your child, ever. Along those same lines, parents need to give kids permission and the tools to trust their instincts. That means if a child feels uncomfortable with someone for whatever reason, the child needs to be taught to tell. Older teenagers need to know that if a date seems to be going in a strange or wrong direction, they can terminate it. We all need to take heart of the sage words of Dr. Judith Orloff of the UCLA School of Psychiatry: "Intuition clears your vision and steers you to the right target."

If you feel uncomfortable or are suspicious of another person's behavior, you should first speak with that person. By letting the person know how you feel, you have communicated, at the very least, your concern regarding your child's safety. Establishing this communication is important because it allows the other person to clear up any misunderstanding or discourages him from committing a future act.

How a person responds can indicate how accurate your suspicions may be. If the person becomes unnaturally defensive or cannot give a reasonable explanation for your concerns, then there is, at least, sufficient reason to be seriously alarmed. Of course, any person who attempts to overly explain his acts should be taken with a grain of salt. When this happens, especially if the other person is a stranger, notify your local law enforcement.

QUESTION 38: WHAT SHOULD I DO IF MY CHILD DISCLOSES SEXUAL ASSAULT?

A *disclosure* is the official term for the statement made when someone says he or she has been abused. How a parent responds is critical to the victim's potential short- and long-term outcomes. Many feelings are aroused, both from the child who discloses and from the person to whom the disclosure was made. *Just remember: a parent's job is **not** to investigate the facts*—a parent's job is to support the child immediately and to quickly get assistance from official resources. During this process, parents are likely to go through a range of emotions—guilt, anger, confusion, doubt, vengefulness, jealousy, and hurt. While the parents must receive individual support later, they must focus first on getting appropriate help for the child.

To be most helpful under these challenging circumstances, you need to do the following:

1. Take your child's disclosure seriously.
2. Report it to the police and child protective services.
3. Participate in the investigation led by a multidisciplinary team of law enforcers, child protective services, and other experts in the field.
4. Reinforce that whatever has happened is not the child's fault and that you are there to protect him or her.
5. Reassure your child that he or she made the right decision by disclosing, whether it was you or someone else who received the initial disclosure.

Here are some things *not* to do after a disclosure (you may wait to take these steps later):

1. Confront the offender.
2. Question your child about all the details.
3. Conduct an independent investigation.
4. Punish your child.
5. State or imply that you don't believe your child.

QUESTION 39: WHAT IF I DON'T BELIEVE MY CHILD?

Always believe your child. Even if a child has a propensity to lie, parents should never assume that a sexual act has not occurred. Sexual abuse is a very sensitive topic, even more so for a child. Therefore, when a child reveals details of sexual abuse, it should never be taken lightly. Children who have been assaulted often fear that they are not believed; parents only add to that fear by ignoring their disclosures. In fact, parents should underreact and should not exhibit disbelief or skepticism. Instead, they should be patient and support their child by letting them know they are believed. Children are not in positions of power and need someone in whom they can confide. If parents cannot trust what their children tell them, whom can children trust?

QUESTION 40: HOW LATE IS TOO LATE
TO REPORT SEXUAL ABUSE?

Two issues determine whether a report will be too late to submit to the authorities. First, there is the legal timeline dictated by the statute of limitations; second, there are social, psychological, and personal timelines.

Legal Timeline

The statute of limitations for sexual abuse cases—the time frame in which charges can be filed—varies from state to state. In some states, there is no statute of limitations; therefore, a victim can actually bring charges against an offender for an incident that occurred decades ago. The recent exposure of sexual abuses by the clergy has only enhanced the public's demand that all states enact legislation that removes time limits on filing charges against a sexual offender. Many people believe that if the goals of the judicial system are fairness and justice, then states should provide their citizens with the right to see their attackers in court.

Those who defend time limits argue that an accused will not be fairly heard because the passage of time will affect his or her memory of the event. They also argue that if the crime were truly serious, it should not have taken an alleged victim many years to report it. In response, proponents for eliminating time limits point out that many victims of childhood crimes do not appreciate the severity of the crime, or they might create a memory block because they do not want to relive the horrific events; in time, they gather the strength and courage to confront their past and to seek punishment for those who had damaged them so long ago.

In California, the statute of limitations for molestation is ten years after the date in which the incident or abuse took place. In 2003, the Supreme Court of the United States struck down as unconstitutional an earlier California law that placed no statute of limitations on molestation crimes so long as charges were filed one year after the victim reported the crime, along with independent evidence to support it. The Supreme Court's reasoning was that it was unfair to defendants that they were not on notice that they could be charged for crimes many years prior. In response to this court decision, the California legislatures simply made a new law that *extends* the statute of limitations instead of reviving the statute of limitations (as it was under the old law). Basically, there is no change from the prior law in that child molestation cases (cases involving substantial sexual conduct when the victim was under eighteen) can be filed within one year of reporting to law enforcement regardless of how many years have passed since the abuse occurred. Still, the law requires that there is independent evidence to support the charges. The legislators in California also found another situation where the statute of limitations can be extended. This is referred to as the "DNA Cold Hits." Statute of limitations can be extended where a victim may have immediately reported, and DNA was found, but there was no suspect to match the DNA to. Under this law, so long as the original DNA was timely analyzed, a case can be filed within one year of the time there was a positive DNA match, which can be years later. There is also an extension of the statute of limitations in cases where a suspect had not been identified originally but later was identified as a result of DNA analysis.

Although criminal charges may not be possible for many victims, all is not lost. Victims may still bring a civil case against their alleged abusers and collect money for any emotional or physical pain. In California, victims of sexual abuse may file a civil case against their abusers at any time before they turn twenty-six. California has even carved out an exception, which twenty-eight states have adopted, that allows an adult who was sexually abused as a child up to three years to bring charges—even if the statute of limitations has expired—against her abuser if she discovers that she has suffered a psychological injury relating to the abuse.

In other states, such as Kentucky, a victim must bring a civil action by either age twenty-three or no more than five years after the abuse had occurred. Many state statutes allow victims of sexual abuse by the clergy to come forward and collect huge settlements. While it may not give the victim the type of justice he or she seeks—jail time for the offender—settlements can provide the psychological empowerment they need to move on with their lives.

Social, Psychological, and Personal Timelines

There are many reasons for reporting sexual assault that have little bearing on whether a criminal or civil case can be filed. As we all know, kids don't disclose sexual assault while it happens, for several reasons. This can lead many adults to falsely believe that if an incident was not disclosed immediately, it cannot be brought forward later.

But there is no timeline for personal healing. A victim can still file a report long after the offense occurred. Despite prohibitions on whether a case can be filed, there are legitimate and good reasons to do so:

1. *Other victims.* Because there are usually many other victims per perpetrator, one report can corroborate a case that has been filed, even if the report is beyond the statute of limitations.
2. *An anonymous perpetrator is more dangerous than a known one.* But if you file a report, an investigation will be officially recorded that could affect a perpetrator's ability to get a job, his background checks, and his access to kids.
3. *A report can be a signal to other perps as well as other victims.* When a perpetrator is exposed, other victims may be more willing to come forward.

The difference between filing a case versus filing a report is that the former memorializes the acts, can initiate an investigation, and very often can be used as evidence of prior acts if and when the suspect is arrested or investigated again. Filing a report is done with the police by the victim or some other mandated reporter, whereas filing a case is the prosecutor's decision. Since the victim or reporter does not generally know what it takes to file a case, a victim (or anyone else) should not decide whether a case is going to be filed. The decision to file a case is up to the prosecutor, based on the reasons and factors discussed in questions 71 and 72.

Reporting a sexual assault to local law enforcement or to child protective services is an important step not only in identifying and stopping a perpetrator but also toward healing for the victim.

QUESTION 41: WHO ARE MANDATED REPORTERS AND WHAT ARE THEIR RESPONSIBILITIES?

The job of a mandated reporter is to let authorities know when any form of child abuse or neglect occurs. In most states, mandated reporters include teachers, social workers, physicians, and law enforcement officials. They also include members of other professions, such as clergymen and mental health professionals, who have frequent contacts with and access to children. While many professions are mandated to report suspected child abuse, many jobs do not have reporting requirements. For example, while teachers are mandated reporters, school secretaries are not.

If a mandated reporter fails to report an abuse, he or she may be subject to civil damages and criminal charges. In California, failure to report an abuse may result in a thousand-dollar fine and is a misdemeanor punishable by up to six months in jail. When a report is made in good faith, meaning that the reporter truly believes that the child was being harmed, he or she cannot be prosecuted or fired if it is later found that the report was not accurate. The law does not want to punish people who have good intentions and are trying to protect a child's safety.

When making a report, the disclosure of the identity of the reporter is usually protected. In some jurisdictions, when there is a compelling reason to disclose, the reporter's information must be revealed.

QUESTION 42: WHAT SHOULD I DO IF I SUSPECT A CHILD, OTHER THAN MINE, IS BEING TOUCHED?

If you suspect that a child is being touched, you should report it to your local law enforcement or child-protection agency, even though you are not legally bound to do so.

Perhaps one of the saddest statements made during an investigation is that others had previously picked up the signs of abuse but were too concerned about their own liability and busy schedules to make a report. From an ethical standpoint, it seems obvious that we should report any suspicions about another person's inappropriate acts against a child. However, some of us are so worried about being wrong that we want to avoid having the accused find out who reported him. The law in most states tries to encourage people to protect children and to report suspected abuse. Anonymous reporting to child protective services allows and encourages concerned citizens to make a report without divulging their identity and without having to fear vindictive lawsuits. Be aware that when reporting suspicious behavior to police, you can request that you remain anonymous. The police will then check out your claim. Remember, the last thing you want to do is confront the alleged abuser, as he may be dangerous or aware that you intend to report him, which can make the child's situation even worse or cause the suspect to flee.

When a person does not report suspected abuse, the child's life may be endangered. Children are not in a position of power or, in some cases, are unaware that they are being abused. As adults, we should be responsible for protecting children, even if not our own.

QUESTION 43: WHAT IS THE DIFFERENCE BETWEEN A SCAR AND A POLICE REPORT?

SCAR stands for Suspected Child Abuse Report. It's generated when someone calls child protective services (often called CPS or the Department of Children and Family Services [DCFS]) and reports a potential case of child abuse or neglect. SCAR reports are vital—if there is a basis to investigate a case from a criminal perspective, the DCFS is obligated to make its own report to law enforcement. Each state and county in the United States has a department responsible for maintaining the welfare and protection of children. Any time there is a suspicion of child abuse (whether physical, sexual, emotional) or neglect, people are either encouraged or mandated to make a report.

The biggest benefit in contacting child services is that you can make an anonymous report, which will start the investigation process. Further, the filing of a report (or even just making a call) is based on *suspicion* of child abuse or neglect. Whether or not it truly exists will be discovered later. If the accusation doesn't pan out, you're not legally responsible.

When contacting CPS, callers should keep these points in mind:

- Not every state has a toll-free hotline, or the hotline may not operate on a twenty-four-hour basis.
- If a toll-free (800 or 888) number is available, it may be accessible only from within that state.

Federal agencies on their own have no authority to intervene in individual child abuse and neglect cases. Each state has jurisdiction over these matters, with specific laws and procedures for reporting and investigating. In some states, all citizens are considered "mandated reporters" and must report any suspicion of child abuse or neglect.

Following is a list of toll-free numbers for the states that have them available.

State Hotlines

Alaska (AK)
(800) 478-4444
Arizona (AZ)
(888) SOS-CHILD
(888-767-2445)
Arkansas (AR)
(800) 482-5964
Connecticut (CT)
(800) 842-2288
(800) 624-5518
(TDD/Hearing Impaired)
Delaware (DE)
(800) 292-9582
Florida (FL)
(800) 96-ABUSE
(800-962-2873)
Illinois (IL)
(800) 252-2873
Indiana (IN)
(800) 800-5556
Iowa (IA)
(800) 362-2178
Kansas (KS)
(800) 922-5330
Kentucky (KY)
(800) 752-6200
Maine (ME)
(800) 452-1999
Maryland (MD)
(800) 332-6347
Massachusetts (MA)
(800) 792-5200
Michigan (MI)
(800) 942-4357
Mississippi (MS)
(800) 222-8000
Missouri (MO)
(800) 392-3738

Montana (MT)
(800) 332-6100
Nebraska (NE)
(800) 652-1999
Nevada (NV)
(800) 992-5757
New Hampshire (NH)
(800) 894-5533
New Jersey (NJ)
(800) 792-8610
(800) 835-5510
(TDD/Hearing Impaired)
New Mexico (NM)
(800) 797-3260
New York (NY)
(800) 342-3720
North Dakota (ND)
(800) 245-3736
Oklahoma (OK)
(800) 522-3511
Oregon (OR)
(800) 854-3508
Pennsylvania (PA)
(800) 932-0313
Rhode Island (RI)
(800) RI-CHILD
(800-742-4453)
Texas (TX)
(800) 252-5400
Utah (UT)
(800) 678-9399
Virginia (VA)
(800) 552-7096
Washington (WA)
(800) 562-5624
West Virginia (WV)
(800) 352-6513
Wyoming (WY)
(800) 457-3659

QUESTION 44: WHAT MAKES KIDS DISCLOSE MOLESTATION?

Children reveal abuses for a variety of reasons and in different circumstances. Many disclosures are given to trusted persons such as teachers, counselors, and psychologists. The person to whom the child confides in is one whom the child perceives to be fair, nonjudgmental, noncritical, and nonthreatening. Very often, that person is not the parent, as children tend to want to "protect" their parents. Or they may fear that parent.

A child's disclosure can be planned or spontaneous. Most spontaneous disclosures seem to occur when the child believes someone already knows about or suspects the abuse. For example, someone might make a comment that the child interprets as an awareness of the abuse.

Younger children often disclose accidentally, whereas older children think more carefully about whom they will tell and how much information they will share. An accidental disclosure is when a child tells about abuse in an indirect way. This is usually based on an external factor that brings about the disclosure. For example, a child may watch a television show and see something that incites him or her to make a comment disclosing abuse. A fellow prosecutor in New York, Jill Starishevsky, told me of a time that the disclosure in one case happened after a child watched an episode of *The Oprah Winfrey Show*. When Oprah had said, "Tell a teacher," that is exactly what the child did!

When a child does decide to report a sex crime, it may be after seeing a program on sexual assault, hearing a presentation on the subject, or reading a book about it. Other times, a child may be asked if something is wrong, which could lead to disclosure. Children may also report abuse after someone else they know has revealed a similar situation, whether by the same perpetrator or a different one. For the first time, the child may feel the chances of support and being believed are higher, which makes it easier to disclose. Other reasons children may reveal a problem include when the child wants to protect another child, if pregnancy is a threat, or if there is evidence of physical injury.

Few young people know that certain deeds are criminal or against the law. Consequently, the notion that children report child sexual assault to punish someone or to bring them into the justice system is simply not so.

QUESTION 45: WHAT MAKES KIDS *NOT* DISCLOSE MOLESTATION?

Sexual assault is one of the most underreported crimes in this country. According to the US Department of Justice 2005 National Crime Victimization Study, sixty percent of sexual assaults go unreported.

There are as many reasons why children do *not* tell as there are for disclosure. Child sexual abuse is a covert activity where secrecy is inherent to the act. Children don't disclose sexual assault for many reasons, but *fear* is the leading one. So what are kids fearful of?:

- They are responsible for the crimes against them.
- They are going to be taken away from their family members.
- They are going to get in trouble for telling.
- The offender will carry out his threats.
- They won't be believed.

Besides fear, there are other reasons children don't disclose. Shame and guilt are high on the list—kids feel guilty that they got themselves into the situation, feel they may have consented, and may even feel guilty for having received sexual pleasure from the acts (including ejaculation). They also worry that telling may get the offender into trouble, may put someone in jail, or may break up their family. All these fears are, of course, valid.

QUESTION 46: HOW DO I KNOW IF MY CHILD IS TELLING THE TRUTH?

Young children rarely lie about having been sexually abused. Teens have a bit more of a tendency to fabricate a story of abuse as they are developmentally riskier than younger children are. But you, as a parent, need to trust your instincts, look at the evidence, and consider your child's statement as you would anything else you were told. For example, if your child told you that another child hit him, you would ask yourself the following:

1. Is it possible?
2. Has my child lied about this type of thing before?
3. Are there any marks or indications to corroborate this?
4. Is there a motive for my child to be untruthful?
5. What was my child's demeanor when telling me this?
6. What does my gut say?

Sociologists M. Steller and T. Boychuk created a "validity checklist'" that provides investigators and parents with a tool to assess a claim of sexual abuse. The checklist includes examining:

- *Appropriateness of language and knowledge, given the child's age.* If the child speaks as though coached or seems to be reading a script written by an adult, this would cast doubt on the child's statement. For example, a six-year-old is unlikely to know or use the word *penetration* in his or her regular vocabulary. However, a four-year-old who says, "White guck came out of Daddy's pee-pee" rings true, given the appropriateness of the words and the description.
- *Appropriateness of behavior.* Does the child behave in a way we would expect after disclosing abuse? Are there fear, nervousness, or other physical symptoms of distress? Of course, there are not always overt signs of distress, as some abused children develop coping mechanisms that allow them to answer an interviewer's questions calmly. Behavior needs to be evaluated with other factors. For instance, a child who lies could certainly be fearful, but then these questions should be asked: Why would the child go through the pain of disclosing and lying if it were not true? What benefit does the child get by disclosing a false claim? Also, often the disclosure is false because the wrong perpetrator was identified, while the abuse was true. A typical example is a child claiming to have been raped by a stranger, when in fact the rape was by a relative.
- *Susceptibility to suggestion.* A child's susceptibility to suggestion by the interviewer needs to be taken into consideration.
- *Motivation.* Is the child's motive to report legitimate or questionable? Is there an adult coaxing a child? If so, what might the motive be?
- *Is the act as described physically feasible?* For example, if a child says she was raped and describes an erection, when the alleged rapist is medically impotent, questions would arise about the validity of the disclosure.

- *Consistency of the child's statement.* Are any parts of the statement contradicted by another statement made by the same child? Has the child's story changed when told to more than one person? In a truthful account, one would expect that the key elements would remain the same throughout, while a child might forget some of the less important aspects.

Perpetrators purposely seek imperfect victims. They look for kids who have inherent credibility issues and will be less likely to be believed—they might give a known drug user drugs. This not only makes the sexual abuse easier to execute but also prevents the victim from discrediting the perpetrator in the future. Perpetrators are extremely calculating when it comes to picking a target. As such, they look for victims who have had problems with their parents, who are likely to be disbelieved, or who have low self-esteem—someone the perpetrator can make feel guilty, as if the victim actually caused the abuse.

Instead of looking at imperfections in a child as reasons not to believe them, parents should be aware that a child's perceived weaknesses or problems at home or school actually make the disclosure more credible. Perpetrators love weak witnesses—they're the best victims. The most logical way to assess the validity of a claim of abuse is to review all known information. Don't forget checking your gut response: do the disclosure and the child's account ring true?

QUESTION 47: CAN A MAN OR BOY STILL HAVE AN ERECTION OR EJACULATE IF HE IS FRIGHTENED?

Perhaps the most confusing aspect of male sexual assault is when the victim has an erection or ejaculates. A common myth is that a victim who had an erection or ejaculation was not sexually assaulted. This is based on the false assumption that erection and ejaculation mean that a victim "really wanted it" or consented to it.

The reality is that no matter what the circumstances are, erection and ejaculation are *physiological* responses that may result from mere physical contact or even extreme stress. These responses do not imply that the victim wanted or enjoyed the assault and do not indicate anything about the victim's sexual orientation. Some rapists are aware how erection and ejaculation can confuse their victims—this motivates them to manipulate their victims to the point of erection or ejaculation to increase their feelings of control and to discourage reporting the crime.

QUESTION 48: HOW IS SEXUAL ASSAULT
RELATED TO ABDUCTION?

In many abductions, a sexual assault has occurred or will occur. Child abduction—a serious crime and a type of abuse—is the taking away of a child by another, older person without permission from at least one of the child's parents.

Two types of people kidnap: family and nonfamily members. Family members, usually one of the child's parents, are the most common people who abduct children—usually doing so when there is a custody or divorce proceeding taking place. Nonfamily members can be broken up into two groups: stereotypical abductors and nonfamily abductors. The former are those that most people think of when they hear the word *kidnapper*; these abductors have no relationship or a slight relationship with one of the parents, have kidnapped a child overnight, and are at least fifty miles from the kidnapping site. Their intention is to kill, torture, or hold the kidnapped child for ransom. In contrast, non-family kidnappers may have some relationship (friend, neighbor, boyfriend) with at least one parent, or they can be strangers. These abductors will threaten or harm the kidnapped child and hold the child for at least one hour while demanding a ransom, or they intend to keep the child indefinitely.

Out of these two groups, nonfamily abductors make up the overwhelming number of kidnappings in the United States. In fact, according to the US Department of Justice, only two hundred to three hundred kidnappings are classified as stereotypical, while over fifty thousand fall under nonfamily kidnappings.

Categorizing is irrelevant when considering what motivates kidnappers. According to the US Department of Justice, over half of nonfamily kidnappers and stereotypical kidnappers sexually assaulted their victims. The victims ranged primarily between twelve and seventeen years old. In addition, more than sixty percent of stereotypical and nonfamily kidnappers were motivated by a sexual purpose. This is an alarming statistic and suggests a strong relationship between kidnapping and sexual assaults.

In 2005, Congress enacted the PROTECT Act to respond to the high rates of sexual assaults in child abduction cases. This led to the creation of the Amber Alert program (see question 50), which notifies motorists on billboard monitors and on TV about kidnappings with the potential to seriously harm the abducted child. The law also increased the length of time in which victims can bring charges of child kidnapping against their abductors, up from ten to twenty years.

Parents should know that the investigation of a sexual assault should be handled like an abduction. In both abduction and sexual assault, time can be critical, even if the assault occurred some time ago. Time affects the ability to investigate the event and to ensure that children are safe.

QUESTION 49: WHAT IS AN AMBER ALERT?

An Amber Alert notifies communities, drivers, and cell phone users that a child abduction has occurred. The program involves the cooperation of law enforcement, broadcasters, and transportation agencies to help bring the abducted child back home safely. The Amber Alert is used only (1) after law enforcement has clearly established that a child has been abducted and (2) where it is believed that there is a threat of serious bodily harm to the child.

An alert is usually issued through the media and bulletin boards. Often, television programming can be interrupted by the local news to inform the public of the abduction. News anchors or reporters will give their viewers the abductor's name, a description of his physical appearance, and the vehicle and license plate involved when the abduction took place. Amber Alerts on electronic bulletin boards along the freeway may include a description of the vehicle and the vehicle's license plate number. The presence of these boards also makes it less likely for the suspect to flee the area, based on his fear of being caught.

PART FOUR

REPORTING SEXUAL ABUSE

QUESTION 50: WHAT KIND OF EVIDENCE IS CONSIDERED
"CORROBORATION" OF CHILD SEXUAL ABUSE?

E ssential for any child sexual abuse case, corroborating evidence increases the certainty
that a claim is legitimate. Without it, the criminal case becomes a "he-said, she-said"
situation that is generally not filed by prosecutors' offices. Such cases are not acceptable
because most states have a jury instruction like, "when there are two versions of the incident,
and one points to innocence and the other to guilt, you are to adopt the version that points
to innocence." This reinforces the concept in our Constitution that we are all innocent until
proven guilty. Because the presumption of innocence basically means that in a tie, the case
goes to the defense, prosecutors need something more. The more evidence the prosecutor
has, the faster he or she can prove a case that meets the criminal standard known as *beyond
a reasonable doubt*. (This concept is the subject of more debate than a presidential
election. Inherent in this standard is the prosecutor's responsibility to show that
the facts prove the defendant committed the crime. While there is no requirement
for certainty, it is the highest level of proof in the justice system.)

Corroboration can be very minor, such as evidence that only a victim would
know. For example, in a case of abduction by a stranger, if a victim can describe a
room (the scene of the crime) and has never been to that location before, this
description is considered "corroboration." Types of corroboration include the defendant's prior record of similar arrests, investigations, and convictions; other victims;
medical, physical, and scientific evidence; and the defendant's own statements.

Defendant's Prior Record

Some corroborations reveal previous similar acts by the defendant. It is not necessary for the defendant to have been convicted for those charges. This type of evidence can show the defendant's pattern of sexual behavior, emphasizing the likelihood that he would commit a similar act in the future.

Witnesses offer good corroborative evidence because they can describe the event on an as-seen basis. A witness can also help add details, confirm facts given by the victim, and attack the credibility of the defendant's recollection of events.

Medical Evidence

Medical evidence can indicate that a sexual act has occurred. This type of evidence is important especially in situations where the child is under twelve and the defendant has claimed he never touched or penetrated any part of her body. This is important because many girls under twelve do not even know how sex is actually conducted, and most have not gone through puberty. Therefore, claims that the child may have had intercourse with someone other than the accused will be regarded more skeptically. During trial, doctors and nurses are allowed to testify about what the victim said during the medical exam. Other medical findings that can corroborate a case are pregnancy, genital injuries, nongenital injuries (like scratch marks on the back), and sexually transmitted diseases.

Physical Evidence

Physical evidence is vital in sexual abuse cases and may include clothes that have DNA or bodily fluids on them, a collection of pornography, items on a computer, guns, keys to secret rooms or hotel rooms, items in a car, or anything else that validates a child's disclosure. The very possession of a particular item can corroborate the victim's account of what occurred and the pattern of the defendant's behavior. For example, I had a case where a child said that it always smelled like vanilla when she was raped by her uncle, yet he never put lotion or cream on her. Upon searching the house, vanilla oils, candles, and lotions were found under the bed where she had been raped.

Scientific Evidence

Inherent in sexual assault cases is the potential for bodily fluid or other evidence on a victim or left at the scene of a crime, which is very important to understanding a case. For example, a suspect's pubic hair in the victim's mouth can corroborate oral copulation.

Defendant's Statements

Sometimes, a suspect's own words, if videotaped, recorded, or sworn can be used against him. This evidence is extremely powerful, even if he does not admit to the crime. For instance, a suspect who admits to every single detail of a day or night that the victim described, except for the sexual assault, may be corroborating the victim's version of the events.

A defendant's statements are sometimes obtained through *pretext calls*, recorded conversations usually conducted by the victim or the victim's parents. The objective: to get the abuser to admit to or give information about a crime. Often, the accused utters apologies and words of remorse or even fear. These calls are entirely legal and effective ways to get a suspect's words into the court record.

QUESTION 51: WHAT ARE THE GENERAL STAGES OF CRIME SCENE INVESTIGATION AS IT RELATES TO CHILD SEXUAL ASSAULT?

We live in the *CSI* generation, so much so that lawyers and journalists have even coined a new term, *the* CSI *effect*, which refers to how television shows like *CSI* (*Crime Scene Investigation*) have affected jurors' ability to deliberate and convict in criminal cases. The specific concern among prosecutors and investigators is that the *CSI* watchers will demand more from the prosecution in scientific evidence and will *wrongfully* acquit a guilty defendant when scientific evidence is not available.

Physical evidence in criminal investigations has always played a critical role in solving crime, but never has it been more anticipated by jurors than it is today. And because of the unique aspects of sexual assault cases (e.g., the relationship between suspect and victim, the age of the victim, and the potential for physical evidence), the process by which we seek physical evidence is important for everybody to understand. Like homicides, sexual assault cases offer the opportunity to uncover various kinds of personal evidence, including body fluids, hair, and fibers associated with a particular area, surface, or object. However, just because there is the *potential* for physical and/or scientific evidence, that doesn't mean that it will be present, available, or conclusive.

Physical evidence in sexual assault cases attempts to connect the dots between the victim, the suspect, and the crime scene. Scientific evidence can identify a suspect and confirm penetration but cannot confirm whether a sexual act is consensual. Scientific evidence that leads to medical evidence can confirm whether a victim's account is consistent with the version of the assault that was provided. In my experience, the primary role physical evidence plays is to confirm that sexual contact actually did occur and to determine who committed the act. Regardless of the actual findings, the fact remains that jurors expect and want access to physical and scientific evidence.

Helpful types of physical and medical evidence include:

1. The results of the victim's medical exam
   • presence of DNA
   • injuries
   • live sperm
   • sexually transmitted diseases
   • pregnancy

2. The results of the suspect's medical exam
   • presence of DNA
   • injuries
   • live sperm
   • sexually transmitted diseases

3. The physical evidence associated with a scene of a crime
   • bedding
   • carpet swatches
   • marks on furniture (e.g., beds)
   • presence of weapons
   • items that only the victim and suspect would know
   • condoms, lubricants, or other creams and lotions

The general stages of crime scene investigation include:

1. Law enforcement responds to the scene of the last or most current assault.
2. The scene is protected and secured.
3. A preliminary survey determines whether there is immediately apparent or visible physical evidence.
4. In some counties or states, a crime scene investigator will come to the scene to collect evidence; in other areas, local police collect the evidence.
5. Scenes can be photographed or sketched, with an accompanying narrative description prepared by the police.
6. Evidence is collected, preserved, and documented.
7. Evidence is sent via appropriate packaging and protocol to a laboratory for analysis.
8. The scene is released.

To tie the scene of the crime to the assault, the physical aspects of the crime scene are used with the medical examinations. Although most people know that victims are frequently the subject of medical exams, suspects should be examined, too. The type of evidence available in a medical examination depends on how much time has passed since the most recent abuse incident. The generally accepted rule is that if an incident has occurred within seventy-two hours, then the medical exam should be immediately performed to secure evidence. Even after seventy-two hours, medical exams can show evidence and should always be considered, but acute exams are done within seventy-two hours of an assault.

While the benefits of medical and physical evidence are obvious, people should be aware that most sexual assault cases lack significant medical and physical findings, for many reasons:

1. The abusive acts may not have caused injury. Vaginas are designed to accommodate a penis. That is their function, and they therefore can stretch and expand without leaving any marks, even on a prepubescent child.
2. The genital area heals quickly.
3. Most examinations are not done quickly enough due to delayed disclosure.

The absence of medical evidence should not doom a case, just as the presence of medical evidence does not tell us the exact details of a case. The purpose of medical and physical evidence is to take some of the pressure off the victim and to corroborate the details of a child's sexual assault.

QUESTION 52: WHAT HAPPENS IF THERE IS A SEXUAL ASSAULT DISCLOSURE DURING A DIVORCE CASE?

While many people like to dismiss a disclosure in the throes of a divorce case, it is important that a trained multidisciplinary team assess the charge as it would any other such accusation. Sometimes, one parent tries to manipulate the criminal justice system with a false accusation to gain an unfair advantage in a family law case. But other times, a child may finally feel safe (because he or she is out of the perpetrator's home) and therefore feels free to make a truthful disclosure.

The manipulation of a child's disclosure has actually been given a name: *parental alienation syndrome* (PAS). The theory, developed by the late Richard A. Gardner, MD, portrays the preferred parent (usually the mother under PAS) as an evil alienator who is virtually solely responsible for turning a vulnerable child against the estranged parent (usually the father under PAS). It is commonly believed that allegations of sexual abuse in the context of divorce are epidemic, that most are made by vindictive mothers, and that these allegations are almost always false.

Let me just say that these beliefs are not supported by scientific evidence.

As a matter of fact, one study conducted by Nicholas Bala and John Schuman, two Queen's University law professors, reviewed Canadian judges' written decisions in 196 cases between 1990 and 1998 where allegations of either physical or sexual abuse were raised in the context of parental separation. Only family law cases were considered; child protection and criminal decisions were excluded. The study showed that the judges felt that only a third of these cases involved someone deliberately lying in court and that fathers were more likely to fabricate the accusations than mothers. Of female-initiated allegations, just 1.3 percent were deemed intentionally false by civil courts, compared with 21 percent when the man in the failed relationship brought similar allegations.

To determine what role a divorce has in evaluating a child sexual assault charge, investigators should consider possibilities other than one parent trying to take unfair advantage of another parent. Some reasons, as pointed out by the American Prosecutors Research Institute's "Investigation and Prosecution of Child Abuse," include:

- The abuse may have started after the couple separated and was precipitated by the stress of the separation.
- The offender's motivation may have less to do with sexual propensities and more to do with a desire to punish the other parent.

- The offender may be a parent's new partner or the child of a parent's new partner, and so the abuse did not begin until after the separation.
- The period following the separation may be the first safe opportunity for the child to reveal the abuse.
- The child may also fear the prospect having to visit or live alone with the abuser.
- The nonoffending parent may, for the first time, feel safe enough to make a report.
- The nonoffending parent may, for the first time, be receptive to the child's allegations and willing to offer support.

When there is a divorce or separation, the nonoffending parent should be sure to let law enforcement make the appropriate inquiries as to whether a child has been coached or forced to make false reports of sexual abuse.

QUESTION 53: CAN A POLYGRAPH BE USED TO VALIDATE A CHILD'S DISCLOSURE OF SEXUAL ABUSE?

Polygraph tests ("polys"), voice stress tests, or any psychological stress tests can be a tool used in the investigation of child sexual assault cases. Generally, however, polygraph tests are not admissible in court, as they are not considered scientifically reliable, but there are benefits to using them.

First, a polygraph can be a good investigative tool when dealing with a suspect but not with children. The polygraph was designed for adults and does not take into account children's developmental issues, age appropriateness, or other relevant issues. Subjecting kids to polygraphs sends the message that somehow children are not as credible, honest, or reliable as other crime victims. This can emotionally harm child victims as well as prejudice the community against them. Legislation in California, Colorado, and Illinois prohibits investigators and prosecutors from requiring or even requesting that an alleged child victim be subjected to a polygraph test before criminal charges are filed. And if there is enough evidence to file charges without a polygraph, then children in those states would unlikely ever be subjected to a polygraph exam.

Perhaps the best reason to use a polygraph is the prepolygraph interview, where the subject is asked generic questions and told how the test will work. Often, suspects afraid of being caught in the polygraph will admit to or make a statement that qualifies as an admission, which can obviously be helpful (and admissible) for the prosecution.

QUESTION 54: WHAT IS "CHILD SEXUAL ABUSE ACCOMMODATION SYNDROME"?

Child sexual abuse accommodation syndrome is a legal/psychological term to describe the blending of several reactions when a child reveals sexual abuse. The term was coined by psychiatrist Dr. Roland Summit and is often used in court to (1) corroborate testimony that a child is acting consistently with the claim of family molestation and (2) explain why victims often recant or retract their truthful testimony in family molestation cases.

While people often expect that a child will disclose sexual assault right after it takes place, children tend to delay disclosing, especially in family abuse situations. In fact, children would much rather maintain the status quo than deal with the guilt and blame involved in disclosure.

The child sexual abuse accommodation syndrome consists of the following symptoms and stages through which a child's disclosure will pass: secrecy; helplessness; entrapment and accommodation; delayed, conflicted, or unconvincing disclosures; and retractions. Let's look at these one by one.

Secrecy

Secrecy makes it clear that the act is bad and/or dangerous. Most children are manipulated, threatened, or warned not to tell by the adult perpetrator. Children keep the secret because they feel they would be blamed or would not be believed or that the person they told would not be able to protect them from the abuser.

Helplessness

Children are inherently helpless and subordinate. They are smaller than adults, dependent, and emotionally immature. For all these reasons, they cannot escape from a dangerous situation in the same way adults can. Children are usually overpowered by adults, and they come to believe that they are helpless, so they stop trying to protect themselves. Instead, they may withdraw, go physically limp, or dissociate.

Entrapment or Accommodation

Children who keep their abuse a secret and continue to feel helpless inevitably feel trapped in their bodies and in their situations. To survive and remain sane, a sexually abused child will choose to accept the situation. This is achieved by believing that he or she provoked the abuse and is actually to blame for it, from its beginning to the present day.

Delayed, Conflicted, or Unconvincing Disclosures

Most ongoing sexual abuse is *never* disclosed, at least not outside the immediate family. Treated, reported, or investigated cases are the exception, not the norm. Disclosure usually occurs after an overwhelming family conflict, the discovery of the abuse by a third party, or a child protective agency's successful attempt to reach out to the victim.

Retractions

Children often retract statements that they were abused when they see their worst fears unfolding. As soon as the disclosure is made, the chaos begins. The abuser is often removed from the home; the remaining parent is upset; the child feels that the only way to make everything return to "normal" is to take back whatever disclosure was made.

A delayed disclosure is often used by the defense to discredit the victim and to show evidence of fabrication. Prosecutors, through expert testimony, will then describe the syndrome to explain how it works and how the child minimizing what happened, blame, and denial are symptoms of abuse.

Child sexual abuse accommodation syndrome may help explain common aspects in child sexual abuse disclosure; however, it does not necessarily apply all the time.

QUESTION 55: HOW DO YOU FIND A PREDATOR WHOSE IDENTITY MY CHILD DOESN'T KNOW?

Investigating a sexual assault by a stranger is done much like any crime would be investigated. First, the victim provides as many physical details about the perpetrator as possible, including hair color, eye color, approximate height, weight, build, unusual marks, scars, tattoos, and such. Next, the police may have an artist draw a composite picture based on the victim's description. The composite can be used to compare with other police reports of both known and unknown suspects.

Following the composite, the assigned detective will search both his own agency's police records and others to see if there is a link between the newly reported crime and others, either solved or unsolved. He'll compare the way the crimes were committed, their location, the age of the victims, and similarities of the suspect description. Other reports are also used to see if there is a way to link a serial predator.

Like any other sexual assault case, when there is an *acute report* (one made within seventy-two hours of an assault), a medical examination is done. Most jurisdictions will even extend the seventy-two hours when there is an unknown perpetrator to try to find any biological evidence that will lead to a DNA match. Every sexual assault medical examination features use of a *rape kit*, including swabs from various parts of the victim's body, including genitals, mouth, face, and sometimes hands and feet. Thus, any biological material that does not match the victim's own DNA can then be uploaded into a computer system to see if it comes back with a match. Since DNA samples are required in most states either upon conviction or arrest of a felony or sex offense, the data bank of known sexual offenders grows daily, thus increasing the chances of identifying a person off a *cold hit* (a positive DNA match in a stranger-assault case).

Another source is information kept on registered sex offenders lists. Investigators will often run known sex offenders in a geographic area to see if they match the description and/or modus operandi of the unknown perpetrator. Through the Internet or the local law enforcement agency, parents can access information about sexual predators whom they or their children may not know. Specifically, the Federal Bureau of Investigation (FBI) has a Web site that lists all the known sexual predators living in the United States. However, each state has its own laws regarding the depth of information it may reveal to the public. In California, some offenders are not required to register as sex offenders and will not be listed on the database. For example, a person convicted of statutory rape would not be required to register and therefore would not be on anybody's radar. In addition, sexual offenders are not required to disclose any other crimes they may have committed, as long as they are not the same type they are required to disclose under state law.

It is important to remember that most sexual predators look like you and me. The reason some predators continue abusing is that they are cunning and know how to get away with certain acts. Therefore, when a sexual predator is not required to register, it is often difficult to distinguish who is and who is not a sexual offender. If parents want to be diligent and have the money to do so, they can get the background information of individuals with a criminal history through various Web sites. Then, if they learn that a local individual is a registered sex offender but has not updated his registry information (in California, sexual offenders must update their registration every year), they should report him to the local law enforcement agency.

When information about a past offender is unavailable, the best thing to do is to educate children on how to protect themselves from predators. Although most child victims suffer sexual abuse from people they know, parents should still teach their children about "stranger dangers," such as not talking to strangers who approach them. To combat against strangers with perverse motives, parents should tell their children to always play in well-lit areas and to be accompanied by an adult that the family knows well. Children should always notify a parent when a person, either a stranger or someone the child knows, offers them a gift, touches them inappropriately, or stares at them constantly. Even if these acts appear innocent or unintentional, the safety of our children should always be front and center.

Parents should also be careful about confronting sexual predators. Once a parent finds out where a predator lives, he or she is subject to criminal or civil lawsuits if the information obtained through the registry is used for an illegal purpose. For example, if a parent verbally harasses a sex offender or loiters at his home, criminal charges could be filed on that parent.

QUESTION 56: UNDER WHAT CIRCUMSTANCES WILL CHILD PROTECTIVE SERVICES (CPS) TAKE MY CHILD AWAY FROM ME?

Our society places much importance on the health and well-being of children. One of the clearest indicators of this can be seen in legal frameworks that permit intervention in families when children are abused or neglected.

While the United States prides itself on freedom, privacy, and individual rights, it also recognizes that the government, at times, must participate in raising children by ensuring that parents are fit, properly caring for their children, not abusing or neglecting them, and protecting them from abuse. Today, child protective services (CPS) agencies are primarily responsible for receiving, investigating, and responding to reports of child abuse and neglect. These agencies are usually linked to child welfare departments with broader responsibilities, which include foster care and adoption. Both are typically housed within state or county departments of social services. CPS must intervene when a child's safety is at risk from abuse or neglect. While many people believe CPS's sole goal is to remove children in purported danger, most social service workers will tell you that sometimes this is only a means to an end and not the intended outcome.

The individual employed by social services works with families to help plan and provide services to:

- Enhance every family's ability to provide proper care for and to nurture their children within their own home, community, and culture
- Prevent separation of the child from the family whenever possible
- Preserve and rehabilitate the family
- Provide a stable, permanent alternative placement as quickly as possible for every child who cannot return home
- Reunite children with families as quickly as possible

QUESTION 57: WHOM SHOULD I CALL FIRST IF MY CHILD DISCLOSES SEXUAL ABUSE?

The police should be the first to be called when someone discloses child sexual assault. After taking down all the information, the police must then cross-report (that is, make a subsequent report) to child protective services.

The authorities must be made aware of a child sexual abuse case for a number of reasons. First, it's the only way to be sure that your child and other would-be victims, including members of your own family, can be protected. The second reason is perhaps even more important. By reporting to the police, you are sending the message to your child that he or she matters, is being taken seriously, and has a voice. And finally, by calling the police, you know that the proper people will handle the investigation. You are ensuring that the courts, police, and social agencies are handling a crime that can affect far more people than one victim's family.

While bringing in the police may raise all kinds of issues—fear of retaliation, concern over the court process, and so on—the police are well prepared to get to the bottom of whether an assault occurred and to be sure it is handled correctly.

QUESTION 58: WHAT WILL THE POLICE DO IF I REPORT THE ABUSE?

Initial reports to law enforcement are generally taken by *patrol officers* or *desk officers*, the officers who respond to a 9-1-1 call. They may also be the ones who take reports from people who stop in. Sexual assault reports can make their way to the police from a call to 9-1-1, a walk into the station, or a report made by child protective services. Reports can come from the victims themselves, other family members, friends, concerned citizens, or mandated reporters such as doctors, teachers, or therapists.

If there is an acute report and enough evidence (called *probable cause*) to substantiate an arrest, the police may arrest the suspect immediately. However, since most cases are delayed in disclosure, the police usually opt to investigate before making the arrest. An investigation determines whether a crime was committed and, if so, who is responsible. This begins with a preliminary report where the basic scenario is analyzed—the who, what, and where. The victim interview, which helps determine where to get more information to help corroborate a case, is coordinated with a multidisciplinary team. In many states, multidisciplinary teams—which include law enforcement, social services, counselors, and attorneys—work together to find the most efficient and effective way to interview children. The goal is to ensure that an interview will stand up in court.

The next stages include speaking with all witnesses who may be able to explain facts, put a scenario into perspective, and corroborate the victim's account. Other stages depend on the type of case being investigated. For example, in an assault by a stranger, an investigation into the identity of the perpetrator will be crucial; in a family case, a look at medical and physical evidence may be warranted. Every possible lead should be evaluated to either corroborate a victim's account or reject it. Then, the police investigator will look at the suspect's criminal history and his statement. Just as much as we want to lock up criminals who have harmed innocent children, alleged offenders should also have the right not to be unfairly accused or arrested.

A false accusation may arise when there is a pending divorce. Divorces can be nasty, and so can the parents involved in them. As a result, children may be coached by one parent to discredit the other parent. Other times, the child may be seeking attention or disagrees with strict rules set up by one parent. The police need to approach each case objectively and should not allow their own concepts about sexual offenders affect their investigation.

But when investigators strongly believe that the accused did abuse a child, they should be aware of certain behavior common to most sexual offenders. First, sexual offenders have an obvious reason to lie: to avoid prosecution and jail time. Many are pathological liars and may convince even themselves that they did not commit the crime. Therefore, investigators need to be highly trained for recognizing deception.

A sexual offender may be well read on the law and may admit to things that will classify as a misdemeanor but not a felony. In these situations, police must not let any admission influence how they conduct the overall investigation. The goal is to find out the whole story, not just one or two chapters.

Once the investigation is completed, the police will then confer with the prosecutor to determine if a criminal case can be filed and, if so, with what charges. Then, if the defendant was not arrested at the outset of the investigation, he will be arrested, and official procedures will begin.

QUESTION 59: WILL AN OFFENDING PARENT BE DEPORTED IF IN THIS COUNTRY ILLEGALLY?

Immigration is a sensitive topic for many people. Under federal law, it is illegal for a person from another country to immigrate to the United States without authorization from the US Government, or if given authorization, to overstay his visit.

Procedurally, a parent who is found guilty of a sexual crime against a minor has to serve the entirety of his sentence in a US prison before he is deported. Some US citizens argue that prisons are overcrowded and that paying taxpayer dollars for incarcerating illegal immigrants is unfair. They propose that illegal-immigrant criminals should serve their sentences in their native country. While the debates about illegal immigration continue, the federal government is daily deporting illegal immigrants who commit sexual acts against minors (under eighteen years old). Therefore, the illegal immigrant criminal should prepare for deportation upon release from federal prison.

QUESTION 60: WHAT IF THE VICTIM IS NOT A CITIZEN?

The reality is that a good number of sexual assault crimes are committed against children who are not US citizens. The government has created legislation that allows for these victims and their parents to stay in the United States temporarily. The reason for such legislation is to encourage victims to report violent crimes without the fear of being deported, jailed, or fined.

To qualify for temporary nonimmigrant status, the victim must satisfy four requirements:

1. *The victim must have suffered substantial mental or physical abuse.* This requirement is to ensure that the victim of a nonviolent, petty crime will not take advantage of reporting the crime in exchange for nonimmigrant status.
2. *The victim must have information about the activity being reported.* Without information, it is impossible to arrest a suspect or file a criminal case.
3. *The victim must help the government in its investigation and prosecution of the crime.* A victim cannot obtain nonimmigrant status if she decides later to retract her story or is uncooperative with authorities.
4. *The crime must have been committed in the United States or have violated a US law.* Otherwise, it is useless to pursue any criminal action because it does not violate any US rights. The whole idea of creating a law that protects immigrant victims is not only to encourage the reporting of a crime but to lock up those responsible.

A victim determined to be eligible for nonimmigrant status must apply for a U-Visa certified by an immigration agency. This is to confirm that the request for nonimmigrant status was done with good intentions and that cooperation was satisfied. The key to the U-Visa is that the victim must cooperate with the criminal investigation and prosecution.

Immigrants may not know what a U-Visa includes, and they may still be discouraged from reporting because they believe it would only delay their deportation. While these are legitimate concerns, immigrants should know that the government is on their side when it comes to obtaining permanent residence in the United States. Some rights from having a U-Visa status are:

1. A person can stay in the United States for up to four years.
2. A person can apply for permanent residency after three years, but he or

she cannot live in another country for an extended period and must have lived in the United States for a significant time during those three years.

3. Parents can be included. A child victim, if her parents are in another country, can petition, with the help of an adult, to bring her parents to the United States. It is important to note that in these situations only the victim can petition on behalf of those whom she wants to bring over and cannot be forced to do so without the victim's approval.

Finally, the legislation states that there can be up to ten thousand U-Visas issued each year. There are plenty of U-Visas to go around so long as the report of a crime is done truthfully and fits into one of the enumerated crimes, such as sexual assault crimes. Even if there are more than ten thousand U-Visas issued within a given year, a victim may still file for a petition to be issued a visa for the next fiscal year.

QUESTION 61: WHAT IS A MULTIDISCIPLINARY TEAM?

A multidisciplinary child abuse team is a professional unit composed of representatives from health, social service, law enforcement, and legal service agencies. Together, they coordinate the assistance needed to handle cases of child abuse, streamlining the investigation and better serving abuse victims. They can also ensure that interviews avoid offering suggestions to the child and are not repetitive or unnecessary. A multidisciplinary team can do more combined than each agency can do alone. In short, they're the "one-stop shop" for investigating and prosecuting child sexual assault.

Not every jurisdiction has each representative on the team, nor do all team members necessarily work on all aspects of a case. While working as a group, each member still plays his or her individual role—the prosecutor still files the case, the law enforcement member still leads the investigation, and so on. Coordination allows members to draw on each agency's strengths. For example, by working as a team, the Department of Children and Family Services (Child Protective Services) and law enforcement can jointly decide when is the best time to interview the offending parent, capitalizing on the element of surprise. Combining the agencies' strengths increases the chance of successful outcome and minimizes investigative pitfalls inherent when many departments work on the same project.

In addition, there are the unmatched professional resources for the child, which derive from the combined knowledge and skills of different professionals with a diversity of backgrounds, training, and experience. This variety can help team members—all of whom are passionate about protecting children—devise a customized plan that will make for the best decisions in each case.

Generally, each agency will make its own appraisal to decide how to handle the case, and sometimes there is some overlap in the process. Perhaps the most obvious is the need for all agencies to interview the child victim(s) and witness(es). By working as a team, the group can decide who may be the best person to do that, based on experience, type of case, and professional strengths. The teams that work best are those that know every member's individual role, respect the different objectives of each agency, and are willing to work together to speed up the process.

Though not exhaustive, the following table represents the key roles of each team member:

Law Enforcement	Prosecutor	Child Protective Services	Child Advocate or Mental Health Representative	Medical
Stabilizes crime scenes	Assesses evidence for provability in a criminal case	Determines whether a child should be removed from a home	Coordinates the team in general and usually acts as the point of contact person for the team and the victim	Interprets medical findings for the team
Collects and preserves physical evidence	Determines what (if any) criminal charges should be filed	Determines what type of contact (or no-contact) orders should be made	Provides guidance in interviewing techniques based on child's age, developmental abilities, gender, and emotional state	Performs forensic medical exams
Interviews all other witnesses, including suspect	Negotiates bail, plea agreements, or any other criminal actions	Negotiates visitations with the parents' lawyers	Makes treatment recommendations and gives referrals to the child's caretaker	Preserves physical evidence found during the medical exam
Runs criminal history	Presents the state's case at trial	Presents the state's case in a family law court	May accompany the child to court if the case is filed	Testifies in court as to the medical findings
WHOLE TEAM	Determines an investigative plan that meets the team's overall needs Participates in a coordinated interview of the victim to meet all the team's needs Supports the victim through the process, regardless of whether a case is filed or CPS action is taken			

Though multidisciplinary teams vary from jurisdiction to jurisdiction, the teams that work best are those where members know their roles and a coordinated decision is made as to who will do what. Whatever each team member's role, the goal of the investigation is to determine if a child has been abused and what should be done about it, always keeping the child's best interests in mind.

QUESTION 62: WHAT IS A FORENSIC INTERVIEW?

While no one wants to admit it, the victim interview is the single most important part of the investigation and prosecution process. Children realize this, despite our constant reassurance that it is only one piece of the investigation. The interview leads investigators to other corroborating sources to help file a case. The victim interview answers two key questions: Was a crime committed? Will the victim be able to describe what occurred and to withstand cross-examination, should a case be filed in court?

Most jurisdictions use interview protocols that set up uniform guidelines for every case. The protocols usually determine who will be the interviewer, where the interview will take place, how the information will be recorded, the format of the interview, and who will be present. While there is no single "right" way, it is generally agreed that a uniform interviewing strategy will help ensure a reliable, credible interview process and minimize the defense's ability to attack the interview process, should a case go to trial.

Although interviews vary, most go something like this:

1. *Introduction:* This begins by greeting the child in a friendly way (by name) and telling the child where he is going and where his caregiver will be.

2. *Leading the child to the interview room:* A child is shown the room and usually given a choice of where to sit. If there is a one-way mirror, the child is told about it, including who is observing.

3. *Orientation:* The child will be given an explanation as to why she is being interviewed.

4. *Rapport building:* Small talk and conversation are meant to break the ice and give the interviewer an opportunity to assess the child's ability to answer questions. The idea is to feel confident that the child will later qualify as a witness in court. (To qualify, a child must be able to distin-

guish between a truth and a lie. Old-school interviewers used to ask questions like, "What is the truth and what is a lie?" Modern-day interviewers ask questions to determine whether the child knows the difference between a truth and a lie. An example would be, "If I said your hair is green, would that be a truth or a lie?")

5. *Inquiry about the abuse:* Once the interviewer feels that the preliminary qualifications have been met, the interview turns to the abuse. The exact questioning depends on a number of factors, including who the abuser was, the child's level of comfort, and the ability to disclose about the individual case. Sometimes interviewers will bring out pictures or diagrams of bodies and ask the child to label the body parts. Sometimes anatomically correct dolls are used, and other times children are given blank paper to draw on. What questions and which props are used depend on the interviewer's discretion, combined with the specific circumstances of the child and the case itself. For example, it may be more challenging to use a doll for a child who is easily distracted. On the other hand, a child who has difficulty describing the correct names for body parts may benefit from looking at a diagram or anatomically correct doll. The interview process begins with general questions and then flows into specific questions when necessary:

   (a) *General questions:* The goal is to get children to discuss the abuse in a free-flowing narrative style, with as little interruption from the interviewer as possible. The best interviewers ask simple questions that can be answered in a story form rather than yes/no questions or questions with multiple-choice answers. There are a number of suggestions and guidelines for interviewing children, including special techniques for very young children, developmentally disabled children, and children who may be medicated. Most professionals agree that the most reliable information comes from children in response to, "Tell me about that," or "Tell me more about that."

   (b) *Specific questions:* The interviewer then tries to figure out if there has been physical abuse; asks about possible witnesses or other victims, why there may have been secrecy and fear, and who was involved; and determines where, how often, and how the abuse occurred.

6. *Ending the interview:* The interview is ended when the child can no longer provide new or useful information. Interviewers like the child to leave on a positive note by offering an opportunity to ask questions. My two final

questions are "Is there any question that I didn't ask you that you were waiting for me to ask?" and "Are there any questions that you have for me?"

Following the interview, someone from the team should meet with the parent or caregiver to answer any questions and address any concerns. This should be done in the victim's absence, with a team member providing simple, straightforward information about the next steps.

The key is not to focus on chances for a prosecution but to achieve open, honest, nonsuggestive interviews that will be helpful, whether or not a case gets prosecuted. Further, the process is designed to support the child—investigators, law enforcers, and other team members cannot simply treat a child sexual assault interview like any other interview. It is *not* like any other interview.

QUESTION 63: HOW MANY PEOPLE WILL MY CHILD NEED TO TALK TO?

Parents who suspect that their child has been sexually abused must prepare for a number of individuals who may want to interview them. When a claim of sexual abuse has been registered, the first priority is to protect the child from further harm or anguish.

However, to determine whether abuse has occurred, investigators must find out whether the child is indeed telling the truth. This is not meant to suggest that a child's credibility rests on how well he or she can communicate specific events. We all know that a child's memory can be short, and a traumatizing experience may prevent him or her from revealing the whole truth. It's important that investigators have testimony that helps them believe the child's story so an investigation and possible prosecution can proceed.

Depending on how the crime is reported, the first person a child speaks with is either a law enforcement official or a child protective service employee. The former will most likely arrange an interview where the facts of the crime can be gathered. As in most crimes where a child's interview is important, the objective is to reduce the number of interviews of the victim, which will help prosecutors establish consistency in a future case or trial. It also limits the child from having to recollect and retell his or her horrifying experiences several times. A CPS agent will determine whether there is a sufficient cause for concern and will then report the incident to a law enforcement agency. Employees who work in a child protective agency have a legal duty to protect children and must report any credible complaints of abuse.

After these initial interviews, a child may be sent to a health-care professional to determine whether there are any obvious injuries to a child's private parts, as well as any mental injuries. The medical exam is an important part of every criminal action taken by a prosecutor, making it highly probable that a child will speak with a health-care professional.

Finally, the child's talk with the prosecutor helps determine whether there are enough facts and evidence to charge the accused. Particularly if the child wants to see the abuser incarcerated, he or she needs to speak with a prosecutor. Without such testimony, there can be no case.

Seeing all these interviewers may seem time-consuming and harmful to a child's psyche because of the number of times the story must be repeated. However, in reality, most states have many multidisciplinary teams that coordinate with each other to reduce the number of interviews.

Among those on the multidisciplinary team are law enforcement officials, health-care professionals, child protective service employees, and prosecutors. One reason why a multidisciplinary team works is that it puts all the people involved in the investigation and prosecution of a crime together in one place. Therefore, a child does not have to go from the police station and then to a district attorney's office to conduct an interview; instead, the child can be interviewed with law enforcement officials and prosecutors in one location.

QUESTION 64: WILL THE INTERVIEW BE VIDEOTAPED?

Most likely, yes. Child interviews are important because they give prosecutors a firsthand account of the child's reliability. In the criminal justice system, the local, state, or federal government decides whether there is sufficient evidence and credibility from the victim to charge another person for a crime. By video-taping a child, the prosecution is better able to gauge the reliability of a child's story by evaluating the child's emotions, consistency of facts, and physical injuries, if there are any.

Based on public policy, some jurisdictions also require the use of videotape when interviewing children to protect them from having to redescribe painful events. Most prosecutors and investigators agree that the positives of video-taping outweigh its negatives, such as helping defense attorneys anticipate the child's testimony or discredit the child's story.

Prosecutors may use a videotaped interview to show the consistency of a child's statements. These interviews are usually conducted in safe, nonadversarial places, such as rooms designed to look like a playroom (with small chairs, dolls, etc.). Often, children are more comfortable and less scared to share information that can be highly valuable to a prosecutor's case. Because children appear more natural in these settings, their testimony has more credibility and reliability with jurors. In addition, videotaped interviews give prosecutors the corroborating evidence needed to persuade a group of twelve jurors to convict the offender.

One concern, especially for parents, is the privacy rights of a child who has been videotaped in an interview. To ensure that privacy is protected, prosecutors usually seek orders from a court to keep the child's interview from being held or distributed beyond the scope of the case or trial. Another alternative is for the defense to watch the videotaped testimony in the prosecutor's office. The courts are very sensitive when it comes to protecting children and will ensure that they are protected as much as the law allows.

QUESTION 65: CAN I WATCH THE INTERVIEW?

This is probably one of the most asked questions. Usually, a parent is not present during an interview with a child. Though initially difficult to accept by parents, it's logical once they understand the process. The outcome is not only better for the child but for the case as well.

The parents' role is usually limited to escorting the child to the interview room and being present through the introduction to the key people involved, including the interviewer. Parents are encouraged to be supportive, as children are very sensitive to verbal and nonverbal cues. A child who senses a parent's discomfort may feel even more reluctant and torn during the interview.

Parents are kept out of the interview to minimize any pressure on or prompting of the child—voluntary or involuntary—that may affect the investigative and interview process. Since the goal is to have a clean disclosure without any suggestibility, coaching, pressure, or the like, the best approach is for the victim to speak only to a trained interviewer. And since the parent is unlikely to be present in the courtroom during any testimony from the child, it is better for the team to assess the child's ability to communicate without any outside influences. The interviews themselves are critiqued enough in the criminal process, so there is no reason to subject them to even more scrutiny, especially since everybody simply wants the truth.

Parents, however, should take heart. Multidisciplinary teams—including prosecutors, social workers, and psychologists—are all highly trained professionals who are sensitive to children's discomfort relating to the interviewer's gender, tone, or questions, and they will ensure that the child feels safe and comfortable. In addition, by working together during the interview, each member of a multidisciplinary team can ask follow-up questions that may lead to the discovery of the truth.

QUESTION 66: WILL MY CHILD NEED TO HAVE A MEDICAL OR PHYSICAL EXAM? IS IT INVASIVE OR PAINFUL?

Medical exams can provide key evidence, such as how an assault occurred, and often reveal physical or scientific evidence on the victim.

Since juries are so conditioned to expect scientific and physical evidence, an investigative team would be remiss in not pursuing an exam. Clearly, the best type of evidence would be a physical injury that corroborated a victim's words. However, there are other benefits of a medical exam, including finding hairs, fibers, DNA, or other scientific evidence. A medical exam can also show that the findings are consistent with the victim's account. Plus, it also shows how serious both the investigative team and the victim were in disclosing the abuse from the beginning.

Parental consent is not required for a medical exam of a child who might have been abused. Representatives from child service agencies or local law enforcement can authorize an exam even if a parent refuses to do so.

Generally, medical exams are not painful because the procedures are safe and noninvasive. For example, the colposcope is a binocular optical instrument used to magnify the genital area to assess the extent of the damage. The colposcope does not touch the child, even though it is equipped with a light and a camera.

Medical and physical exams are important because they can provide powerful evidence for prosecutors in criminal cases. Because children do not usually provide the full story of the acts committed against them, medical exams can help investigators better understand and reveal the severity of the child's injuries. Prosecutors and investigators are aware of any pictures of the child's genitals or other body parts taken during the exam. To minimize the embarrassment and unwanted exposure—either for investigative purposes or for use during trial—procedures are in place to protect the child.

Medical exams can also help doctors diagnose any sexually transmitted diseases or traumas a child or parent may not be aware of. Doctors also have the opportunity to educate and counsel the child regarding the damages—emotional, physical, and psychological—that he or she may have suffered. Finally, medical exams can effectively negate the argument by defense attorneys that there is not enough evidence to bring a charge against their clients.

PART FIVE

GOING TO COURT

QUESTION 67: HOW DO YOU DETERMINE WHETHER A CHILD CAN TESTIFY IN COURT?

Before even determining whether children must go to court, which essentially means they will be subpoenaed to court, it needs to be determined whether they will actually qualify to testify. Case law and the evidence code of each state usually dictate the requirements any witness must meet to qualify to testify in court. Interestingly, most courts make the determination based not on age but on the witness' ability to participate in the court process.

Certain questions must be asked. For a child to be considered competent and able to testify, the judge must feel the child knows the difference between right and wrong. In other words, the child must understand the difference between telling the truth and telling a lie and must recognize and agree to tell the truth in court.

In defining a lie, most adults will say, "Something that is not true." But the concepts of truth and lies can be personal and difficult to define, even for sophisticated adults. For young children, attorneys and judges have found simple ways to lay the groundwork to determine competency. See the following example.

Attorney Questioning a Three-Year-Old
Q: How old are you?
A: Three.

Q: If I said you were ten, would that be the truth or a lie?

A: You're silly. That would be a lie.

Q: Do you know your colors?

A: Yes.

Q: What color marker is this?

A: Red. [Correct answer.]

Q: What color marker is this?

A: Blue [Correct answer.]

Q: If I said this marker was yellow, would that be the truth or a lie? [Marker held up is red.]

A: A lie.

Q: Have you ever told a lie?

A: Yes.

Q: What happened?

A: I got in trouble.

Q: What was the lie?

A: I told my mommy I brushed my teeth when I didn't.

Q: When you are in court, you are going to always need to tell the truth. Is that something you can promise to do?

A: I promise, pinky promise.

In this case, the child would likely qualify as a witness because the child could give answers, could identify the difference between a truth and a lie, and knew that there were consequences for telling a lie.

In sexual assault cases, many states require that prosecutors and judges take into account the victim's desire to prosecute. The most powerful evidence is the child's own testimony. Therefore, although it is not necessary for a child to go to court, the child's testimony can greatly influence the filing or outcome of a case.

Most cases will not get filed without the victim being able to describe the actual acts or assaults that led to the disclosure, but there is an exception. Alternative means are used to describe the crime. These can include accounts from witnesses who observed the acts or at least parts of the acts, DNA testimony (where the recovery of the DNA itself confirms that the abuse happened), or other pieces of evidence combined with the defendant's own statements or admissions.

If the court finds that a child is incompetent to testify—either because she is too young or cannot be relied upon to tell the truth—then the child will be unable to be used as a witness during trial. In this way, the court, not the parent, decides the very difficult issue of whether a child should testify.

Even when the case can be made without the victim's account, my conversations with jurors have confirmed my belief that jurors want to hear from the victim. They want to know what happened in the victim's words so they can make sense of the evidence themselves. I think jurors feel that if a sexual assault victim is not present, he or she must be lying or doesn't care enough to prosecute. (This should be distinguished from domestic violence situations, where the lack of cooperation with victims is quite common and even expected. A victim who does not appear tends to corroborate the control the suspect has over her, which can be seen as proof that the victim is in the cycle of violence.) A child's testimony can give jurors a firsthand account of the traumatic experience. By viewing a crime though the lens of the victim, jurors can evaluate the sincerity of and emotional impact on the victim. Sometimes, prosecutors do not have sufficient corroborative evidence to convict a sexual offender; however, a child's testimony may help link corroborative evidence, making it significantly stronger than it might have been without the child's testimony.

Children generally make good witnesses because they have no motive to lie. Although children do lie when they are with their peers, lying about serious crimes is rare. Usually, the court allows testimony of a child unless there is good cause to believe that a child is lying or has a habitual propensity to lie.

To reduce a parent's concern regarding a child's testimony, prosecutors and child specialists have adopted specific procedures to better prepare children. For instance, prosecutors may allow a child to sit in an empty courtroom so that she can be familiar with the courtroom and all its gadgets before she testifies. A prosecutor may allow the child to speak in the microphone or may tell her to sit in a witness chair. Sometimes, a prosecutor may ask the child to answer the same questions the prosecutor will ask in trial. This helps ensure that the child will not be intimidated by certain questions and will be prepared for the trial.

If the child is uncomfortable pointing out the offender or being in front of a courtroom during testimony, the court has arranged ways in which the child will not have to be in direct view of the accused. Witness chairs may be exchanged for a miniature chair to accommodate a child who feels intimidated by an adult chair. The court will often grant requests for breaks after every fifteen minutes of testimony by a child who is five years or younger. In some situations, a support person can help with the child's emotional well-being during the testimony. When this happens, the support person, such as a social worker or a psychologist, may assist in questioning the child to help her feel more comfortable answering specific questions.

QUESTION 68: WHAT IS THE DIFFERENCE BETWEEN CRIMINAL COURT, CIVIL COURT, FAMILY COURT, AND DEPENDENCY COURT?

For many people, especially those not familiar with the legal world, understanding the different courts in the legal system can be confusing and frustrating. Mostly, the differences between each are procedural, but understanding these is essential for parents who are seeking to send their child's offender to jail, while at the same time obtaining custody of their kids or suing the offender to obtain monetary judgment for any harm he may have caused the victim and the victim's family.

Criminal courts decide what the reasonable punishment and expenses should be for the crime the defendant has committed. The court's objective is to hold the defendant responsible for the acts he commits and accordingly punish him. Of course, punishment cannot be carried out until a jury, or in some cases a judge, has been convinced beyond a reasonable doubt that the defendant is guilty.

The standards of proof in criminal cases differ substantially from those in civil courts (explained below) because the latter require only that the defendant, more likely than not or by a preponderance of evidence, has committed the offense claimed by the plaintiff. Therefore, a person may theoretically be found not guilty of a crime under criminal law and found guilty under civil law. In practical terms, this means that a person may be liable for money damages for the harmful or negligent acts he committed, without having to serve any jail term for those offenses. A criminal court can punish a guilty person in a number of ways, including jail sentences, fines, and probation.

Another important point is that prosecutors act as agents for the state and government in criminal cases; the government's goal is to serve the public's interest by keeping criminals from engaging in repeated activities that may harm other people in the future. Therefore, offenses brought under criminal law are often seen as crimes against society.

Civil courts decide on issues of dispute between two or more private parties. Usually, these disputes are not criminal but involve issues dealing with contracts, property rights, and negligent behavior. It is different from a criminal court because the dispute usually involves an offense that was committed against another individual and not society.

Family court is a type of civil court that seeks to resolve issues of family disputes, including custody rights, child-support payments, visitation rights, restraining orders, and mandated counseling. Only parties who are legally married to, divorced from, or related by blood to the defendant can bring a dispute under family court. A family member may also choose to bring an action under criminal court while seeking to obtain rights under family court.

Dependency courts focus on children's well-being, protecting them from abuse and neglect that may have come from their parents. Dependency courts are not criminal courts and therefore do not have the power to impose punishment. Their role is to do the most they can to strengthen families so children can live in homes where safety and neglect are not an issue. However, in situations where significant abuse and neglect are present, criminal charges may be brought against the parents, and children are usually placed in protective custody. In a subsequent court proceeding, the judge will decide whether the child should temporarily or permanently live with a foster parent or adoptive parents.

QUESTION 69: WHAT RIGHTS DO VICTIMS HAVE FROM GOVERNMENTAL AGENCIES?

Most states have some sort of "victim's bill of rights," which describes the specific responsibilities that law enforcement and prosecutor's offices owe to the child victim in the investigation and prosecution of a sexual assault case. Most victim's bills of rights are not necessarily for sex crimes, but they apply to any victim brought into the criminal justice system.

The key to the criminal justice system is to ensure that there is open communication between the victim (and family) and the prosecutor and law enforcement agencies. Communication serves to explain confusing and difficult times that may occur both in and out of court.

To get a sense of what rights states give to victims, I have listed some of the rights that seem to be consistent from state to state, though the actual verbiage may change:

1. To be treated with fairness, respect, and dignity, and to be free from intimidation, harassment, or abuse, throughout the criminal justice process.
2. To be informed, upon request, when the accused or convicted person is released from custody or has escaped.
3. To be present at and, upon request, to be informed of all criminal proceedings where the defendant has the right to be present.
4. To be heard at any proceeding involving a post-arrest release decision, a negotiated plea, and sentencing.
5. To refuse an interview, a deposition, or other discovery request by the defendant, the defendant's attorney, or other person acting on behalf of the defendant.
6. To confer with the prosecution, after the crime against the victim has been charged, before trial or before any disposition of the case and to be informed of the disposition.
7. To read pre-sentence reports relating to the crime against the victim when they are available to the defendant.
8. To receive prompt restitution from the person or persons convicted of the criminal conduct that caused the victim's loss or injury.
9. To be heard at any proceeding when any post-conviction release from confinement is being considered.
10. To a speedy trial or disposition and prompt and final conclusion of the case after the conviction and sentence.
11. To have all rules governing criminal procedure and the admissibility of evidence in all criminal proceedings protect victims' rights and to have these rules be subject to amendment or repeal by the legislature to ensure the protection of these rights.
12. To be informed of victims' rights provided by each individual state.

The specific rights regarding victim compensation, protection of privacy, and right of support people are discussed throughout this section.

QUESTION 70: WHAT MAKES A CASE QUALIFY TO BE FILED?

Filing a criminal case is one of the most important functions of a prosecutor (also known as a deputy district attorney, an assistant deputy district attorney, the state's attorney, the county attorney, or the city attorney), who decides whether a crime has been committed and, if so, which charges to file.

The highest level of proof required in a criminal case is "beyond a reasonable doubt." There must be enough credible evidence to warrant filing the charges (short-term objective) and for a jury to convict the defendant (longer-term objective).

Prosecutors need to evaluate two main elements when determining whether a case should be filed: (1) whether the victim is believable and (2) whether there is sufficient evidence to go forward. "He said/she said" cases are generally not filed because the defendant is always presumed innocent until proven guilty. (This means that, by law, if there is equal weight between the prosecution's evidence and the defense's theory, the benefit will go to the defendant.) Therefore, to tip the scales and find the defendant guilty beyond a reasonable doubt, prosecutors insist on having some evidence that will corroborate, or support, the victim's claim. A victim's disclosure alone would not be enough for a case to be filed.

"Corroboration" is anything that substantiates or adds weight to the victim's disclosure. Evidence that can count as corroboration includes:

- DNA residue
- medical evidence, including injuries consistent with the report
- the defendant's confession, admission, or statements
- the defendant's criminal record or prior conduct, whether or not convicted
- pretext calls (calls the victim made that resulted in statements that give credibility to his or her claims—which are completely legal and admissible)
- other victims of the same perpetrator
- information that only the victim would know (e.g., unusual scars on the genitals of the suspect, what a room looks like that they would not otherwise know)
- other witnesses, including people the victim immediately disclosed to who can corroborate the first disclosure

No matter how tempting it may be to simply file a case, a prosecutor must ensure that it can be proved in court. Factors a prosecutor will consider are:

1. Has a crime been committed?
2. What crime was committed? (Which penal code section is involved?)
3. Who committed the crime? (What's the identity of the perpetrator?)
4. What connects the defendant to the crime? (What kind of corroboration is there?)
5. What defenses are available? (What will the defendant say?)
6. How strong is the witness's testimony? (Can it be corroborated?)

It does no one any good to file charges simply for the sake of filing charges. It is more traumatizing to any victim, but particularly a child, to bring charges and then see the defendant found not guilty.

QUESTION 71: WHAT HAPPENS IF A CRIMINAL CASE IS *NOT* FILED?

A prosecutor who decides that a case cannot be prosecuted as given has three options: to request further investigation, to reject the case, or to refer the case to another agency.

Further Investigation

Seldom are cases immediately ready to be filed. Because child sexual assault cases require some corroboration (see question 71), the detective must provide it through further investigation. More research may lead to more information and evidence that will help prosecutors win their case in court.

A case can be filed anytime within the statute of limitations, which is generally longer for child sexual assault crimes than for other crimes. In California, for example, the general statute of limitations is ten years. So long as the clock is not running out, it is advisable for law enforcement and the prosecutor to take enough time to investigate and to build a strong case. Of course, unnecessary delay does not help since it's rarely to the prosecution's benefit.

To Reject the Case

Prosecutors must reject or decline to file charges if, after reviewing all the available reports and evidence, they have determined that either a crime was not committed or that a case is not provable beyond a reasonable doubt. A rejected case can be reopened in future if the necessary evidence becomes available and the statute of limitations has not expired.

To Refer the Case to Another Agency

If there is a more appropriate way to handle a case other than to file criminal charges, the prosecutor may refer it to another agency. Often this is referred to as *in lieu of*. For example, if a suspect is on probation or parole when the crime was purportedly committed, the prosecutor can decide to end the probation or parole on the old case instead of filing new charges. This is done because the standard to demonstrate such a violation before a judge is a lot easier than proving to a jury that the defendant is guilty beyond a reasonable doubt. A defendant can be on probation or parole for anything when he violates the terms of his release. Therefore, a person on probation for a driving under the influence (DUI) case can have his probation revoked based on the existence of a reported sexual assault case, without even having new charges filed.

Probably the most common referral is when the crime itself does not amount to a felony. For example, a case where a child was patted on the buttocks may qualify as a lesser misdemeanor as opposed to a felony charge. In jurisdictions like mine, where felonies and misdemeanors are generally handled by a different agency (for example, the county prosecutor handles one and the city attorney handles the other), the case may be referred to another agency to file the misdemeanor. The same is true in federal cases. Sometimes, conduct that may be handled by either the state or the feds may be cross-referred from one agency to the other (i.e., the feds can refer to the state and the state can refer to the feds).

QUESTION 72: WHO FILES A CRIMINAL CASE AND WHAT CAN BE CHARGED?

A big difference between child sexual assault cases and other investigations (even adult rape cases) is the team approach to the investigation, prosecution, and handling of a criminal case. (See question 62 for more information on multidisciplinary teams.) Regardless of who interviews the victim, the criminal case is filed by the prosecutor after receiving it from the police detective.

The law breaks up sexual abuse into categories based on a combination of the following criteria:

- the specific sexual act
- the intent of the person doing the act
- the age of the victim
- the age of the perpetrator

Generally, most states have a statute known as *lewd and lascivious acts*, under which any touching of a young child (usually under fourteen) combined with sexual intent is considered per se criminal and by extension also sexually abusive.

Lewd and lascivious acts with a minor is probably the most frequently charged and most generic of all child sexual abuse charges because it is relatively easy to prove the following:

- that the victim is under a specific age
- that there was some sort of sexual touching
- that the intent was to excite, arouse, appeal to the prurient interest, and so forth

These elements are relatively straightforward because sexual touching shows the intent. The only time intent really becomes an issue is when there is some accidental touching (like rubbing past someone or accidentally brushing against a breast) or when the touching is for a nonsexual purpose (for example, bathing, applying medicine, assisting with bathroom needs). But frankly, what other intent can you see other than sexual when an adult orally copulates with or fingers a child?

For something to be lewd and lascivious, touching does not necessarily need to be on the sexual organs. Some states allow for lewd and lascivious acts to be filed even if the touching is on a nonsexual organ, so long as the touching is combined with sexual intent. For example, an adult who rubs a child's arm and says, "I want to have sex with you," can be charged with lewd and lascivious acts.

Some states also have the equivalent of a lewd and lascivious act section when there is a particular age difference between the victim and the perpetrator. For example, in California, if the victim is fourteen or fifteen and the suspect is ten years older, then a version of lewd acts with a minor can be charged as well.

Statutory rape (also known as unlawful sex with a minor) is usually filed in cases where the victim is between fifteen and eighteen (the exact ages vary from state to state) and the perpetrator is over eighteen. Even in cases of consensual sexual intercourse, due to the age difference, the victim does not have the legal capacity to consent, and such an act is therefore against the law. (In question 5, I discuss consent in more detail.) Statutory rape is considered abusive to make sure that adults are held accountable for their actions. If a child results from consensual intercourse, as a prosecutor, I want to make sure that the child will be supported and properly cared for. In some situations, prosecuting a case as a statutory rape will ensure that the father will take financial and parenting responsibility for his offspring.

Sexual abuse is defined as "any sexual assault or sexual exploitation by another person." A *sexual assault* is the unlawful touching of another person's private parts, which is not limited to touching the flesh; it also includes touching outside layers of clothes. A person who sexually assaults another must have the intent to satisfy his or her own arousal. When there is no lewd or lascivious act statute, or when the victim doesn't qualify as a minor (meaning the child is not young enough), then sexual abuse is defined by the acts and how they are accomplished. Sexual acts accomplished by force, fear, duress, undue influence, intoxication, fraud, or other illegal means are considered sexual abuse.

Sexual exploitation is the conduct of a person who demonstrates an intent to distribute, sell, or prepare obscene material to or about a minor. Sexually exploitative acts also include acts in which one responsible for a child's welfare knowingly takes pictures or allows others to take pictures of a minor participating or engaging in an obscene act. Put simply, sexually exploitative acts are those by a person who uses pictures, video, or any other tools to exploit sexually suggestive poses or sexually explicit acts for profit or personal use.

QUESTION 73: HOW LONG DOES A PROSECUTOR HAVE TO FILE CHARGES?

The length of time a prosecutor has to file charges is referred to as *the statute of limitations*. A prosecutor must make sure a case is investigated and filed within this time frame. It's always best to investigate and file cases as soon as possible because no prosecutor, detective, or victim benefits from an unnecessary delay. However, a case should be filed only when the investigation is complete.

Each state's unique statute of limitations lays out the time limit for each crime, how the clock runs, and how to get an extension. Most states have a general statute of limitations for all crimes and then specific exceptions and requirements for crimes that may warrant special treatment, such as sexual assault. Legislators have recognized that sexual assault victims often delay their disclosure—sometimes, for many, many years. Given that reality, combined with the recidivism rates and dangers of sexual predators, the statute of limitations for child sexual assault cases is significantly longer than for any other crime, besides murder, by as much as ten to fifteen years, depending on the state.

In California, for felony charges, the general statute of limitations for child sexual assault cases is ten years. An extension can be granted in cases where the identity of the perpetrator was unknown until a DNA sample came in or when there was "substantial sexual abuse" with corroboration of the victim's disclosure. The corroboration cannot be the testimony from a psychologist that the victim was abused; however, it can be the defendant's statements, or those of other witnesses, or multiple victims.

While virtually every jurisdiction limits the time in which general felony charges can be brought, some states (Kentucky, North Carolina, South Carolina, Virginia, West Virginia, and Wyoming) have no limit on felony child abuse charges. Charges can be brought at any time, regardless of when the crime might have occurred. To determine the statute of limitations, consult your state's penal code to find the general statute of limitations, then determine if there is an exception for a sexual offense against children that extends or removes the limitation. (Nearly all states do.)

QUESTION 74: WHAT IF THE VICTIM OR PARENT DOES NOT WANT TO FILE CHARGES?

It is not unusual for people to merely report that a child was touched and thus feel that they have fulfilled their legal, ethical, and civic responsibilities. While coming forward to law enforcement is certainly commendable, people must realize that many possible routes follow the filing of a police report.

Criminal cases are different from civil cases because the former are filed by the state, county, or city and against the named defendant, in this case, the molester. The victim, often referred to as the *complaining witness* by the defense, is *not* a party in the lawsuit and therefore not the person bringing charges against the perpetrator. As such, it is not the victim's choice as to whether a case should be filed.

The reality, however, is that prosecutors want to work with the victim to obtain a conviction. To determine the best result, prosecutors should consider the victim's wishes. For example, in many of my cases, I find that victims don't want the defendant to go to jail but do want to see him registered as a sex offender or in counseling. Sometimes the only way to achieve this is for the case to be prosecuted, which will ensure that the defendant will get the help he needs.

The biggest concern in filing a case is not what type of sentence the perpetrator will receive. It's the victim's desire not to have to go to court and testify in front of the defendant. As I discuss later, some cases can be proved without the victim actually going to court. Defendants who plead guilty and accept responsibility for their actions save the victim the pain, agony, and inconvenience of going to court. No prosecutor wants to see a victim reveal painful experiences to a judge or jury. However, often the decision of how a case will proceed is in the hands of the defendant. If he chooses to deny, lie, or refuse to accept responsibility for his actions, going forward with a criminal prosecution is sometimes the only way to send the message to predators that they can't get away with assaulting children. Similarly, the only way to protect other potential victims is to either get the defendant registered or to get him locked up.

QUESTION 75: CAN A PARENT FILE A CIVIL CASE?

Parents have a right to file civil actions against the perpetrator. The legal standard of proof is lower in civil cases than in criminal cases. Therefore, even if a suspected child abuser is acquitted of all criminal charges against him, he may still be liable for any financial or medical damages if a jury finds that he is guilty of the alleged offense under a civil case.

However, prosecutors encourage parents not to file a civil suit until the criminal case has been resolved. Prosecutors do not want any testimony or evidence in the civil case to contradict the testimony or evidence in the criminal case. If a civil case has already been filed, parents are encouraged to avoid any depositions until the criminal case is finished.

Can a child sue? To file a civil lawsuit, a person must be of *legal capacity*—which is different from the need to be competent to testify—as required by law. To testify, the child must be able to show that he or she can participate in the court process by answering yes to the following questions:

- Can you understand the difference between right and wrong?
- Can you understand the difference between telling the truth and telling a lie?
- Are you willing to take the oath and promise to tell the truth in court?

People do not have legal capacity to sue until they are eighteen. The law treats children as if they are disabled. While this may seem unfair to child victims, adults are thus unable to bring a legal action against them. The theory is that children are protected from the court system because they do not have the knowledge or experience to function in the complex world of court cases and litigation.

QUESTION 76: CAN MY CHILD'S IDENTITY BE SHIELDED?

Many states, including California, Illinois, Iowa, Louisiana, Michigan, Texas, New York, and Washington, have laws that give prosecutors the authority to keep the victim anonymous in court documents. In lieu of using the child's name, the prosecutor can refer to the child as "Jane Doe" or "female child age nine." Even if a state does not have a specific law that authorizes the shielding of the child's identity, a prosecutor can always place a motion in court asking for the court's permission to do so. This protects the child from information that may become public record and thus be available to the media or the outside world.

Although the child can be anonymous for purposes of public record, a child's identity cannot be shielded from the defendant. A criminal defendant has a constitutional right to know who his accuser is. In the event of a trial, the defendant would also have the right to confront and cross-examine witnesses against him—if he represented himself, he would have the right to ask the witness questions when presenting his own defense. Anonymity rarely becomes an issue, as most perpetrators know the identity of their victims. As a matter of fact, I often explain to victims that the defendant usually knows much more about them than I do. For example, if the defendant and the victim have a father-daughter relationship, the father not only will know who she is, but will also remember the time she stole bubblegum from a convenience store, the test she cheated on, and so on, which can destroy her credibility.

QUESTION 77: ARE COURTROOMS CLOSED IN CHILD SEXUAL ASSAULT CASES?

Out of all the laws relating to child sexual assault, the one that has the most variance is in whether courtrooms are allowed to be closed during the criminal prosecution.

Keeping a courtroom closed is rooted in the protections provided to Americans under the United States Constitution, specifically the First Amendment, which gives the press and public access and the right to attend a criminal trial. The second basis is within the Sixth Amendment, which guarantees the accused a "speedy and public trial." Despite federal limitations, several Supreme Court decisions have given courts some leeway in closing the courtroom so long as various factors are met:

- The party seeking to close the courtroom must show that there is an overriding interest likely to be prejudiced unless a court is closed.
- The closure must only seek to address the interest in factor (the specific fear or concern of the child) and not be overly broad (meaning the courtroom cannot be closed for every witness in a child sexual assault case).
- The judge needs to consider reasonable alternatives to closing the proceeding.
- The judge must state the reasons for closing the court on the record.

Some states have actually enacted laws that authorize the judge to close a courtroom during a child sexual assault case, but others require proof of necessity. Three states (Florida, Georgia, and Massachusetts) insist that courts be closed when a child is testifying in a child sexual assault case.

While criminal cases require a case-by-case analysis in determining whether a courtroom can be closed, in civil litigation, often courtrooms are closed to the public and the press. Although trials in family court are usually open, judges have authority to close the proceedings when children testify.

QUESTION 78: WHAT ARE THE TYPICAL STAGES OF THE CRIMINAL COURT PROCESS?

The following stages occur in the court process as related to sexual assault.

Stage 1

A crime occurs. In the realm of child sexual assault, this is the molestation. The police are notified because a disclosure was made by a victim to the police, a mandated reporter, or someone else (like a parent) who contacted the police.

Stage 2

An arrest is made, sometimes immediately upon filing the police report. Other times, an investigation occurs prior to the arrest. This decision, usually made by the police, depends on:

- how recently was the crime committed
- how much immediate available proof there is (called *probable cause*)
- whether the suspect knows about the police involvement or disclosure

Stage 3

An initial bail is set for the charge(s) that the suspect is arrested on, but the amount can change depending on what charges the prosecutor actually chooses to file.

Stage 4

The arraignment is the first court appearance, where the defendant is formally informed of the charges that the prosecutor filed. When the defendant is in jail (meaning he did not post bail prior to the filing of a case), the arraignment is held shortly after the arrest. In California, that period is within forty-eight hours from the time of arrest.

At the arraignment, the defendant will need to decide whether to plead *guilty* or *not guilty*. In most sexual assault cases, the defendant does not plead guilty at the first appearance because the defense attorney has had little or no opportunity to do an investigation to determine how a case should be settled. Also, the consequences of a guilty plea in sexual assault cases include lifetime ramifications (e.g., sex offender registration) and defense attorneys want to ensure that their clients are competently represented. A *not guilty* plea at arraignment does not mean that the defendant won't ultimately plead guilty. The judge will also review the defendant's bail and set dates for future proceedings.

Stage 5

At the preliminary hearing or grand jury indictment, the prosecutor generally brings criminal charges in one of two ways: by a *bill of information* (secured at a preliminary hearing) or by grand jury indictment. In the federal system, cases must be brought by indictment. States, however, are free to use either process. Both preliminary hearings and grand juries are used to establish probable cause. If there is no finding of probable cause, a defendant will not be forced to stand trial.

A preliminary hearing is like a "mini-trial," where the prosecution simply needs to prove that the defendant should be held accountable for particular charges. Witnesses come into court to answer questions from both the prosecutor and the defense attorney, and a judge (not a jury) determines if there is sufficient evidence to make the defendant stand trial. In cases filed without a grand jury, courts want to be sure there is at least probable cause to keep a defendant in custody while awaiting jury trial.

A grand jury, which serves for a year, listens to evidence presented by the prosecutor to justify the filing of a criminal indictment. The grand jury may call its own witnesses and request that further investigations be performed. The "indictment" is the title of the document with the list of charges when the grand jury decides that there is sufficient evidence to try a defendant in court.

Stage 6

Pretrial motions are arguments by both the prosecutor and defense attorney to determine what evidence will be admitted at trial. The determination is made by a judge.

Stage 7

At trial, witnesses testify to prove a defendant guilty of charges beyond a reasonable doubt. If the prosecution cannot prove the case beyond a reasonable doubt, the defendant is entitled to a not-guilty verdict on that count. In a trial, the defendant has the right to call witnesses to support his claims of innocence and is entitled to cross-examine the prosecution's witnesses.

In a jury trial, twelve members of the community determine if the defendant is guilty beyond a reasonable doubt; in a court trial, the judge decides. All twelve jurors must agree on whether the defendant is guilty. Following a guilty verdict, a defendant will be sentenced by the judge.

Stage 8

In plea bargaining, the prosecution and the defense negotiate to settle a case rather than continue it in the courts. It can only be done in criminal cases. An offer in a plea bargain is generally made by the prosecutor after assessing the strength of the case, the defendant's rap sheet, the harm to the victim, the likelihood of conviction, and the minimum and maximum sentencing options. The idea is that going to trial is a risk—anyone can be on the jury, so any outcome is possible. Therefore, to minimize the risk for both parties, the prosecution might offer the defendant an incentive to resolve a case early. This saves further expense, inconvenience to the witnesses, and the need to prove the charges beyond a reasonable doubt.

Stage 9

During the sentencing phase of a criminal case, the court determines the appropriate punishment for the convicted defendant. To arrive at a suitable sentence, the court will consider a number of factors, including the nature and severity of the crime, the defendant's criminal history, the defendant's personal circumstances, and the degree of his remorse.

A defendant on probation may be sentenced to the local jail rather than to the state prison or penitentiary. *Jail* and *prison*, although used interchangeably, are really two different places. The most notable difference is that prison inmates have been tried and convicted of crimes, while those in jail may be awaiting trial. A prison is under either federal or state jurisdiction, while the jail houses people accused under federal, state, county, and/or city laws. A jail holds inmates from two days to a year. If someone is given jail time as a part of his probation, most often, he serves it in the county jail. (*Prisons* and *penitentiaries* are the same.)

When released, the defendant has a period in which he has certain terms and conditions imposed on him by the court, including paying fees, going to therapy, registering as a narcotics or sex offender, doing community service, paying restitution, and checking in with probation. A violation of any term or condition is considered a violation of probation and could subject the defendant to the maximum time.

Once a defendant is released from state prison, he is often put on parole, which is similar to probation. Terms and conditions are imposed on the parolee, which, if violated, can send the parolee back to state prison. In California, defendants found in violation of parole can spend up to one year in jail for each parole violation.

Stage 10

Appeal: An individual convicted of a crime may ask that his or her case be reviewed by a higher court. If that court finds an error in the case or the sentence imposed, the court may reverse the conviction or find that the case should be retried.

* * *

While the preceding represents the phases of the criminal procedure process, a case may not go through each stage. Cases can end at any time if the decision is made to settle the charges either by a guilty plea, acquittal or hung jury, or dismissal of the charges by a judge or prosecutor.

QUESTION 79: HOW LONG DOES THE
CRIMINAL PROCESS TAKE?

One of the most frustrating aspects of the criminal justice system for victims and family members is how long it takes from filing a case to its conclusion. While there are specific constitutional rights to a speedy trial for the defense and the prosecution, both parties can waive these rights and request more time.

As a prosecutor, I try to see that cases get tried as quickly as possible. To me the only thing that gets better with age is fine wine. The passage of time usually serves only to assist the defendants, not the victims. Witnesses' memories fade; witnesses and victims move or leave the area; evidence can get lost or misplaced; and people lose interest, excitement, and the motivation to go forward. Despite these drawbacks, no one (prosecutor or defense) should go to trial until they are prepared to do so. Very often, cases are delayed pending DNA results, psychological tests, or other evidence that may resolve a case, short of a full-blown jury trial.

So as prosecutors, defense attorneys, and judges weigh the requests to continue cases, they all should be mindful of the downside. They must also be realistic about what is needed to resolve a case. A case in which there is no doubt that it will go to trial should be vigorously pursued from the beginning by both parties.

QUESTION 80: HOW DO YOU PREPARE A CHILD
TO TESTIFY IN COURT?

Jurisdictions vary as to how to prepare a child for court. In general, two aspects must be handled: preparing the child and preparing the parent or caregiver. Both child and parent need to know what to expect. The child will look to the adult before court for answers and reassurance. Then, when the focus is on the child, parents will understandably be tense and in need of reassurance as well.

Children should be told at the filing stage that when the time comes (if it comes) for them to attend court, they will have the chance to learn about court, know what to expect, and ask any questions that they have. By informing them that *court school*—preparation and an overview of the process—precedes any court date, children and parents can feel at ease that they won't be plucked from their respective homes out of the blue to go to court.

In court school, children and parents have time to get reacquainted with their "team," as well as an opportunity to learn about the court process, what to expect in court, how to handle questions, and tips on dealing with concerns that have arisen. While the substance of the court orientation should be similar for both parent and child, each should be oriented separately. The theme that caregivers, attorneys, therapists, and others should hold paramount is that "knowledge is power." The more (age-appropriate) information kids have about the process, the better they will fare before, after, and during court. The same goes for parents. Adults should be briefed about who can (should) come to court, what to expect, how to be supportive, what to wear, and so forth. This enables parents to speak the same language as the multidisciplinary team, which can field questions when they arise between court school and the court date.

When the time comes to subpoena a child for court, prosecutors generally try to personally contact the parents before they've even received the subpoena. By doing this, parents and their child can be invited to an in-person meeting to prepare both the child and the parent for the court process.

The information that both parents and kids need to know includes:

1. Which people will be present in the court? The likely possibilities are:
   - the prosecuting attorney
   - the defense attorney
   - the bailiff
   - the court clerk
   - the court reporter
   - the judge
   - the defendant
   - the investigating officer or detective
   - the jury (and jurors)
   - a support person (or advocate)

2. which people will likely *not* be present in court (e.g., certain family members)
3. what a courtroom looks like (e.g., pointing out where each person sits in the courtroom)
4. when the results of the trial or hearing will be known and who will inform them
5. other timing issues

- how long the child will be on the stand
- the preparation for continuances or delays
- who will wait with the child and parent prior to testimony
- the definitions of recesses
- what to do if a break is needed

6. special rules for trials
   - not to speak to other witnesses (define who they are)
   - being careful of what is said in the hallway
   - circumstances when the child may need to return to court

QUESTION 81: WHAT SPECIAL PROCEDURES ARE IN PLACE FOR CHILD SEXUAL ASSAULT VICTIMS IN COURT?

Courts have taken into consideration that child victims may need special accommodations if required to testify. While each state varies regarding the specifics, certain ways are universally recognized that make the courtroom more approachable, less intimidating, and more child friendly. Accommodations can include:

1. *Timing.* Children tend to have much shorter attention spans and cannot focus on one subject over a long period. To prevent intense, multihour testimony from children, courts have the authority to allow for children (particularly those under eleven) to testify during normal school hours.
2. *Comfort.* For the court process to feel more homey or comfortable, children can be permitted to bring a stuffed animal, a "blankey," or some other security object to the witness stand. Water and tissues can be and should be made available.
3. *Privacy.* There are certain ways to ensure privacy for the child from the public, especially the media (but not the perpetrator). First, minors are never referred to by their first and last names. If their name is used at all, it can be shortened in court documents to the first name and last initial, such as "Robin S." Children can also be referred to as "John Doe" or "Jane Doe." Another privacy issue is closed-circuit television, which could allow a victim to testify outside the presence of the perpetrator. Closed-circuit television, though seemingly the perfect solution to

easing a child's fears, is not always available. Each state has specific requirements and many hurdles to using this technology. In addition, there are also issues of whether the technology is even available for courts (and prosecutors) to use.

4. *Court layout.* Courts can be modified to take on a more informal feeling. For example, courtroom personnel can be rearranged so they sit in different locations (say, around a table), or the judge could even hear the case "off the bench" and at a lower, more visible level, closer to the child. Judges can also take off their judicial robes while a child testifies. Other laws involve the procedure by which kids actually testify—how they will be asked questions, how they must respond to questions, and child-sensitive ways to deal with objections. Prosecutors can request from the judge digression from the regular rules of evidence to ask the child questions in a sensitive and appropriate fashion. While a child still needs to be able to qualify as a witness, requests and objections can be made to ensure that questions are *not* asked in a harassing style and that vocabulary can be geared toward the ability of the child to understand it. Attorneys may even be able to lead the child witness if it will assist the process.

While the options to modify court procedures are numerous, the goal is to be sensitive to children and their needs. A study by the American Psychological Association in 1984 reported that the traumas for children are intensified because the court process does not give them any rights. By adapting courtrooms to children, we show them that they do matter and that their well-being warrants making accommodations and changes to the normal court protocol.

QUESTION 82: IF A CASE IS FILED, WILL MY CHILD NEED TO TESTIFY IN COURT?

This is probably the single most asked question by parents to prosecutors. It's often accompanied by dread, angst, and fear, which is totally understandable. Parents and caregivers who are distraught and feel helpless often put their energy into protecting the child from testifying. But this protection is often misguided and can wreak havoc on a criminal case.

A defendant has the right to go to trial and the right to confront and cross-examine witnesses against him. Since the prosecution has the burden of proving a case beyond a reasonable doubt, witnesses, including the victim, will need to be called to the stand.

Jurors want and expect to hear from the victim. The victim's own words and recitation of what happened makes a case stronger and has greater impact than almost anything else. So if a case goes to trial, a victim would need to testify.

Most cases, however, settle through plea bargaining well before a case goes to trial. Often, defendants prefer to take a sentence that has a potential for life out of custody than risking many, many years or even life in prison. In determining whether a case should be settled, one factor prosecutors look at is whether the child testified and how the child did on the stand.

Sometimes victims also need to testify at preliminary hearings or at grand jury hearings. A preliminary hearing occurs when a prosecutor files a complaint rather than an indictment. Because the law would not allow people to simply be put in jail for no reason, a preliminary hearing allows a judge to decide if there is enough evidence to warrant holding the defendant to answer for the charges against him. In some states, a preliminary hearing requires live testimony from all the witnesses; in others, it can be done by hearsay testimony (a police officer testifying for the victim based on earlier interviews). Even in jurisdictions that allow for hearsay, the preference is to have the victim testify, for several reasons. One, it gives the child a dry run of what the courtroom experience is like, without being in front of a jury. Two, it allows the prosecutor to see how the child will do on the stand and how he or she will respond under cross-examination. Third, it is an opportunity to get a sneak peek at the defense's case to see the issues before a case gets to a jury.

But the best reason is the same benefit that occurs in a trial: the chance for the victim to see that he or she can confront the abuser. This alone can greatly contribute to the child's healing process.

QUESTION 83: IF MY CHILD HAS RECEIVED A SUBPOENA, WHAT HAPPENS NEXT?

There is nothing that gives parents (and children) more anxiety than a subpoena requiring the child to testify in court. But there is a clear sense of empowerment as soon as everyone leaves the courtroom.

The main thing that witnesses must remember is to always tell the truth, even if the truth is "I don't remember." If I could tell my witnesses the next five most important things about testifying in court, they would be:

1. Listen to the question.
2. Answer the question and no more.
3. Use simple words and don't agree with words you don't understand.
4. There is nothing to memorize. A case is your experience, so just say what happened.
5. Don't guess your answers.

Of course, I have many other suggestions for how to be an effective witness in court. There is something comforting about having a comprehensive list right in front of you when you need it, such as:

- *Appearance:* Dress as you would for church or an important job interview.
- *Objections:* If a lawyer objects, stop talking and wait for the judge to rule. If the judge says, "Overruled," that means you can answer the question. If the judge says, "Sustained," that means the attorney must ask you the next question, so don't finish answering.
- *Breaks, restroom:* If you need a break, just ask, no matter where you are in the proceeding.
- *Mistakes:* If you feel you made a mistake in your earlier testimony, before you get off the stand, ask if you can correct it. At least that will alert your attorney that there is something you want to say on the record.
- *Manner:* Be calm, courteous, and respectful to both lawyers and the judge. Try not to become angry or frustrated. Cross-examination is a part of every trial. Beware of the lawyer that tries to bait you and get you to lose your cool.
- *Answering:* Use words that can be transcribed by a court reporter. To have a clear record of the proceedings, do not substitute words with nods, uhs, yeahs, and arm movements.
- *Silence:* If there is a moment of silence, don't feel compelled to fill in the empty space.
- *Jurors:* Do not communicate with jurors and do not talk about the case in the hallway, as there may be other witnesses or jurors in earshot.

Anybody testifying in court may feel nervous. But after a few moments, most witnesses realize that they are recalling something that they've experienced and talked about before. Just make sure you remember to take a breath and then answer the questions honestly and directly.

QUESTION 84: CAN'T MY CHILD JUST WRITE OUT A STATEMENT OR TESTIFY VIA CLOSED-CIRCUIT TV?

Closed-circuit television testimony can be broadcast to jurors, judges, and attorneys in a separate room. Usually, courts will not allow closed-circuit testimony unless the child would feel traumatized by the presence of the defendant. If the child's discomfort in testifying comes from just being in the courtroom, courts are less willing to grant prosecutors the use of closed-circuit testimony.

Many states allow children to testify through a closed-circuit television. For prosecutors, each advantage of closed-circuit television has a corresponding disadvantage. One advantage is that it allows the child to testify without ever confronting or seeing the perpetrator, protecting the child from being traumatized by the defendant's presence. However, the child's testimony does not have the same emotional effect as in-person testimony would have. Also, in states where the defendant is allowed to be in the same room as the child, testifying in front of a jury may be actually less intimidating than a taped testimony. Another disadvantage is the possible misuse of electronic equipment to broadcast a child's testimony. Sometimes, such mishaps can be sufficient for a judge to declare a mistrial.

A written statement of testimony is also known as an *affidavit*. This is sworn testimony that is usually given when a witness, which may include a victim, cannot or chooses not to appear in a courtroom. The same concerns that prosecutors have about video testimony also apply to written statements. For example, jurors cannot get an intimate look at the victim to gauge his or her truthfulness. Written statements also eliminate the powerful testimony a child victim may offer for the prosecution's case.

QUESTION 85: CAN I WATCH MY CHILD TESTIFY?

There are some situations in which a parent will be allowed to observe a child testify, but there are others when, though not prohibited, I believe that parents should not.

Most jurisdictions allow for a support person to accompany a child to hearings that are critical or potentially stressful during the criminal prosecution process. For example, in California, the penal code lets victims have "advocates present at any evidentiary, medical, or physical examination or interview by law enforcement authorities or defense attorneys." The preference among professionals is to use advocates who staff a crisis center, the district attorney's office, or the police station. This is not meant to discourage a victim from pursuing his or her own support system, but to help prosecutors do a better job should a case go to trial. A parent not only is *not* the preferred support person but can undermine the process. There are specific scenarios—such as when that parent has witnessed the abuse—when a parent may not be allowed to be the support person, *whether or not* a child wants the parent in the courtroom.

In general, I believe that the presence of a parent (or any caregiver) at either the investigative interview or the actual criminal court case should be strongly discouraged. A parent's presence can bring up a variety of issues that risk discrediting the integrity of the investigation and/or testimony. For example, a parent who scratches her head after a question is asked may appear to be signaling the child when in fact that head scratch can be a perfectly mundane and normal behavior. There is no reason to add a layer for questionability, and keeping an interview clean from potential misinterpretation or suggestiveness is the preferred practice.

The presence of the parents can also open up the common defense tactic that the child is being pressured to disclose or to testify. Any tiny motion, glance, or gesture can be construed as nonverbal communication intended to affect the testimony. Even if the defense attorney does not directly attack the parent's involvement, a juror might draw the conclusion that the parent's presence is an undesirable factor in the courtroom.

Children often do not want their parents to be in court. Frequently, parents do not know the exact extent of the abuse, and children want to "protect" their parents from knowing all the facts. Therefore, child sexual abuse accommodation syndrome (mentioned earlier, in question 55) is likely to rear its head, with the victim denying and minimizing the abuse to preserve the parents' comfort level.

Finally, it's always unwise to let the child victim decide who should be present. Children expect the "good" adult to tell them what is correct and why. The child should, at this point, already have a positive relationship with a team of experts who can assist as support persons in court.

I tell members of multidisciplinary teams to simply inform parents that they are not encouraged to attend court proceedings. This is to take the pressure off the child, which is more important than possibly bringing a parent problem into the court.

Ideally, through the investigative process and court processes, the parent and members of the multidisciplinary team should all be in regular communication where this type of reasoning is explored and explained. By doing so, any issues between the parents and the team will be resolved so that child victims do not have to navigate their way through a conflicted relationship.

QUESTION 86: WHAT ARE THE TYPICAL DEFENSES IN CHILD SEXUAL ASSAULT CASES?

While proving a child sexual assault case can be complex, there are relatively few available defenses. The most common strategy is showing that the prosecution could not meet its burden of proving the case beyond a reasonable doubt.

In a typical sex crimes case, the defendant exercises his right to trial because he feels he has nothing to lose by testing his fate on a jury. The prosecutor must prove the case beyond a reasonable doubt for the defendant to be found guilty. The defendant is willing to take a gamble on the jury or judge because, if he's found guilty, the potential sentence or plea includes so much jail time.

When a defendant goes to trial under these circumstances, the defense strategy is to muddy the prosecutor's theory of the case, question the evidence, raise issues with the victim's credibility, and throw out lots of red herrings and smoke screens, hoping that the jury will bite. The defense will bring up as much "dirty laundry" as possible to get the jury to dislike the victim, ruin her credibility, or paint a picture of a liar, a troubled child, a drug user, or anything else that works. Often victims (and prosecutors) get nervous about people who come off as bad witnesses. Victims are worried that their past drug use, consensual sex, poor grades, mental health issues, or anything else will destroy them and their case.

In a perfect world, the victim will have a comfortable enough relationship with the prosecutor to share the things that may come up that seem bad for the case. As I have said before, knowledge is power, especially for the prosecutor. As the prosecutor, it is always better for me to know the good, bad, and ugly about all the people in the case. Particularly in child sexual assault, I know that very often the defendant knows far more about the victim than I do. To the extent that information can come out in advance, it does tremendous good for a case. Anything bad can be dealt with. For example, if I know that my victim had lied in the past, it is much better for me to bring it up myself in the opening statement and get it out there, rather than for me to not know and have it sprung on me and the jury.

I had a wonderful professor in law school who called this technique *pricking the boil*. Any perceived weakness can be spun into a positive. Take drinking or using drugs as an example. If I know in advance that the victim had been drinking, not only can I be the one who brings it up and "pricks the boil," but also I can later prepare a case showing that *of course* a predator would pick the drunk girl as opposed to the sober, more stable girl. So, yes, the defense is going to try to muddy and victimize the victim. That's why the best plan is to be ready to show that this victim is consistent with those selected by a calculated predator.

One benefit of criminal law, and in sex crimes specifically, is that it is usually easy to spot the arguments and positions the defense is likely to take. Besides the fact that most of the evidence going to trial is turned over in the legal process known as *discovery*, making both prosecution and defense aware of the evidence, there are only so many ways to paint a sex crimes case. The arguments are rather predictable, with the following being the most common when it comes to disputing the credibility of the victim:

1. The child is lying because of the delay in reporting.
2. The child is lying because she has disclosed more and more as time has passed.
3. The child is lying because she minimized, denied, or recanted the allegations.
4. The child misperceived or misunderstood the defendant's behavior/actions.
5. The child has a history of poor behavior and therefore cannot be trusted or believed.
6. The child was coached by the other parent, as there is a divorce/custody case going on.
7. The child was coached and bullied by overzealous prosecutors, police, advocates, or other members of the multidisciplinary team.
8. The child fantasized or dreamed about what happened.
9. The defendant is a good guy—an upstanding member of the community, an involved parent, with no prior record, etc.
10. The child is lying to get attention or because the rules of the house are too strict.

Predictable defenses mean that the prosecutor can prepare in advance how to overcome them. The prosecutor (and victim) will not be upset by them but will be prepared for the likelihood that they will come up. After all, the defense has to say something! Although I have actually had cases where the defense was, "I was walking up the stairs, and my penis just fell into my daughter's vagina. It was crazy"—those cases are usually few and far between. These ten items are really the only things that the defense can say in cases where consent is *not* at issue.

Good prosecutors will know the strategies to refute these defenses. Sometimes this includes calling expert witnesses to explain child accommodation syndrome and discuss why child sexual assault victims disclose the way they do. Perhaps more important than refuting the defense is the prosecutor's ability to appeal to the jurors' common sense.

Besides picking on the victim, there are two other common defenses in sexual assault cases: "not me" and consent. "Not me" is when the perpetrator says, "I didn't do it. Someone else did." The defendant is usually not denying the act; he's just saying he's not the one responsible. Yet very rarely is identity an issue in child sexual assault. Because the victim and perpetrator usually know each other, it is difficult for a defendant to say that the victim is mistaken as to the perpetrator. However, this defense is popular in "stranger danger" cases. The "not me" argument is usually refuted by DNA evidence, the testimony of other people putting the defendant at the scene, prior similar acts, or the defendant's own statements.

Another defense, although limited, is consent. It's available only for the crimes in which the law allows the victim to consent. Consent doesn't have a place in the cases where the law clearly states that a child under a certain age is unable to consent. Consent is the key defense in rape cases, but not in statutory rape cases.

Question 87: What Is Jessica's Law?

Jessica's Law is the name of a 2006 Florida law that mandates longer sentencing guidelines and requires lifetime GPS tracking devices for people convicted of sexually assaulting minors who are twelve years or younger. Over thirty other states have adopted similar legislation that makes it harder for first-time sexual assault offenders to get a lighter sentence or to be free from any restrictions once they have served their sentences.

Jessica's Law is named after Jessica Lunsford, a nine-year-old girl who was murdered by a convicted child molester. In response to the public outrage regarding the state's soft mandatory sentencing guidelines for child molesters, the Florida legislature passed Jessica's Law and made it the toughest legislation on sexual assault against minors in the country. The law requires a twenty-five-years-to-life sentence for any person who molests a child twelve or younger. Even after finishing their sentence, convicted child molesters are either put on probation or under community control for the rest of their lives. Moreover, a monitoring device is placed on the convicted child molester to help law enforcement detect any activities that may endanger the safety of children.

Jessica's Law was designed to punish sex offenders and reduce repeat offenses, but new evidence suggests that the residency restrictions are pushing more sex offenders onto the streets without reducing recidivism.

QUESTION 88: DOES THE VICTIM HAVE A SAY IN THE PERPETRATOR'S SENTENCING?

Because prosecutors choose which charges will be filed, they have a great deal of control in how a case may be handled. When I teach detectives how cases are filed, I instruct them in filing/sentencing as suggested by Deputy District Attorney Cathie Stephenson: "What you charge is a function of what you want the outcome to be."

So what does that mean? Prosecutors, not judges, have the first say in how they want to shape a case, which determines how aggressively they want to pursue it. For example, certain charges carry mandatory minimums, which means no matter what a judge or jury personally thinks, if a defendant is convicted of a particular charge, he must be sentenced to that time, period.

There are two ways in which someone can be convicted of a sex crime and then sentenced: by plea bargain or by conviction following a trial. Just as prosecutors have the authority to decide what cases they want to file, they also have the discretion to *plea bargain*; that is, to change, dismiss, or add charges as part of an agreement before trial, where the defendant will plead guilty or no contest in exchange for a predetermined sentence. Depending on the case, a prosecutor may seek short- or long-term jail sentences or simply ask for probation against the alleged offender.

Procedurally, the judge decides on the sentencing of the convicted offender. The prosecutor, after obtaining a conviction, recommends an appropriate sentence. Some jurisdictions have mandatory sentencing guidelines for some offenses—which judges need to follow—that automatically determine how long the offender's sentence will be. For crimes without specific guidelines or crimes that range in the number of years that can be given, prosecutors must consider a number of factors and bring them out during sentencing to help the judge determine what the fairest punishment should be. Factors include but are not limited to:

- what the safety of the community will be if the defendant is released
- what physical, psychological, and emotional harm the defendant's act has caused the victim
- whether the defendant is willing to pay restitution for the victim's medical costs
- whether punishment will act as a deterrent on people who have considered or have already committed sexually abusive acts against a minor

Without understanding the impact of the defendant's crime on the victim, the victim's family, and society, judges may hand out sentences that do not accurately reflect the harm actually caused. Therefore, victims and their families can play an indirect role in sentencing by giving an *impact statement*. During sentencing, the victim and her family may attend the court proceeding and present an impact statement to communicate the tangible and intangible effects the defendant's actions have had on them. Sometimes, these statements are very powerful and can influence jurors to sentence the defendant to the maximum number of years legally allowed. This statement can also help judges become more aware of the overall impact of the crime. If the victim is uncomfortable or unwilling to make a statement, she can still write a letter that can be read aloud in trial. Also, when the defendant is a family member of the victim, family court will decide whether the victim and her family may be granted the right to be spared any further contact with the defendant upon his release.

Although impact statements are useful, prosecutors also look into the defendant's history of violence, the nature of the act against the victim, the defendant's acknowledgment of guilt, and the defendant's level of desire for treatment. All these factors help prosecutors to recommend the most effective punishment that will help the victim and society to live in a safer community.

QUESTION 89: WHAT ARE THE USUAL SENTENCES/ PUNISHMENTS FOR SEX CRIMES?

Sentencing and punishment vary from state to state. However, criminals who commit sex crimes generally receive longer sentences than criminals who commit other felonies. When the victim is a child, the sentencing is even longer.

A battle is raging between legislators, who want mandatory sentencing for offenders who commit sexual acts against minors, and people who believe that punishment should be flexible and reduced if the offender is able to rehabilitate successfully. For instance, some states are proposing twenty-five-year mandatory sentences for offenders—regardless of whether it is a first-time offense—who commit a sexual assault against a minor thirteen or younger.

Sex crime sentencing varies depending on the age of the child and the type of act committed. Criminals who sexually assault minors twelve, thirteen, or fourteen years or younger, depending on the state, receive longer sentences than if the victim were fourteen or older. In California, the sentencing guideline for a lewd act on a child is three, six, or eight years in prison.

Once a jury convicts the offender, the judge has the final say on sentencing and punishment. In some cases, the criminal may have used a weapon or threatened the child with serious harm. Many states will treat these crimes as more serious than if no threat was used and will add more years to the punishment.

Another issue is whether each act is considered a separate charge when a child victim has been touched or sexually assaulted more than once. Prosecutors usually make the final decision; if they believe that there is not enough evidence for each act, they will charge the defendant for the crime that was committed over a certain period. The defendant may have committed multiple types of crimes during this time, such as touching and forcible rape, which may increase the number of years of his sentence. Specifically, in California, each act of molestation results in a sentencing between three and nine years. When a child is kidnapped and then molested, the kidnapping charges add another five to eleven years. If the defendant has committed statutory rape, under California law, it is considered a misdemeanor if the act was consensual and the other person was less than three years younger than the defendant. If the victim is three or more years younger, the crime is punishable for up to three years.

Many times, criminals are given a reduced sentence, subject to parole, if they can show good behavior or can be shown to be rehabilitated from their desire to harm children. Many critics argue that sexual molesters or people who commit crimes against minors cannot be rehabilitated. They believe that a sexual desire to be with a child is incurable and fear that releasing molesters into the community will only put more children in harm's way.

QUESTION 90: IS REGISTERING AS A SEX OFFENDER A LIFELONG REQUIREMENT?

In a word, yes. By law, sex offenders must register once they are released from prison, and they must update their registration, within five days, each time they relocate to another address. For example, in California, a convicted sex offender is required to register as a sex offender with a local law enforcement agency. Sex offenders must update their registration every year. In some cases, when the crime committed is considered violent, sex offenders must update their registration every ninety days.

Controversy has followed this requirement, as not all crimes are violent or involve the same intent to commit a crime. For example, an eighteen-year-old male must register as a sexual offender if he is prosecuted and convicted for having sexual intercourse with a seventeen-year-old female, who cannot legally consent. Proponents of mandatory registration legislation respond by saying that there are consequences for every action. They claim that nonviolent offenses, such as possession of child pornography or solicitation of a minor for sex, are only treated that way because the offenders were prevented from executing a more serious crime they would have committed had they not been caught. Perhaps a middle ground is the best solution. One proposal would be to clearly define which types of acts are considered nonviolent offenses so that offenders for nonviolent crimes will not lose their rights unnecessarily.

In 1996, Megan's Law (see question 8) was enacted. It required states to implement programs that mandated law enforcement agencies to notify the public about any sexual offenders who may pose a threat to the community. Megan's Law is named after Megan Kanka, a seven-year-old girl raped and murdered by a convicted child molester who had lived right across the street. Megan's parents pushed for legislation that would inform the public about any sex offenders living in their own communities. As a result, Megan's Law is now in every state in the country.

In some states, such as California, parents do not have to look up information about sex offenders at their local police station. Instead, they can access that information through their computer, without ever leaving the comforts of their own home. Included in these Web sites are a map and an address of the sex offender's current residence and descriptive information that includes the sex offender's previous sexual violations, height, weight, and picture.

QUESTION 91: CAN CHILD VICTIMS GET A PROTECTIVE ORDER OR RESTRAINING ORDER?

Yes. Usually, obtaining a protective order involves no cost. Anyone can obtain a protective order as long as the person can show the court that an abuse is ongoing or that there is a threat of bodily harm.

There is much confusion regarding the difference between a protective order and a restraining order because people often describe both interchangeably. A protective order is a court order, issued in civil court, protecting individuals from being abused, harassed, or contacted by an abuser or a stalker. A protective order can do several things: it can order the offender to stop any communication with the person seeking the order, order the offender to keep a certain distance from another person, and prohibit any physical abuse against the alleged victim. Any violation will result in jail time or fines, determined by the language written in the order. Only when abuse is significant and obvious will a prosecutor decide to file criminal charges against a person who is brought to court for protective-order purposes. Typically, a protective order will protect only a person who is related to the abuser and not those who are unrelated, such as strangers. Persons considered to be related are husbands, boyfriends, adults related by blood, parents, and children.

In contrast, a restraining order is a civil order usually related to issues regarding child custody, divorce, and paternity, but the effect is still the same. A restraining order may stop the husband or ex-boyfriend from contacting or communicating with his wife or ex-girlfriend. A common characteristic in both types of orders is what is being protected—people who have been physically abused and want to protect themselves from further harm or threats. In these cases, the issue is safety.

However, there are also different types of restraining orders. A harassing restraining order, for example, is usually less specific regarding what the offender can and cannot do. For instance, in Minnesota, a harassing restraining order does not specify how far an offender should be kept away from an alleged victim of abuse. The harassing restraining order does not deal with any custody issues, mainly because these orders are sought against people who are unrelated to the victim. Therefore, people—especially celebrities—often seek protection from stalkers or harassers using this type of order.

Usually, once an order is given, its effect will last until the next court appearance, which is usually two weeks. This is called a temporary protective or restraining order. At the person's next court appearance, a court will decide whether to cancel the order or make it permanent, lasting up to five years in some cases.

In most states, it is customary that a protective order automatically be filed with the court upon the filing of a criminal case. This helps to put defendants on notice about what behavior is unacceptable and inappropriate.

QUESTION 92: WHAT HAPPENS IF MY CHILD OR SOMEONE ELSE RECEIVES THREATS FROM THE PERPETRATOR?

Prosecutors and judges regard intimidation or threats to a witness involved in a criminal prosecution very seriously. So should victims, family members, and the perpetrator himself. Threats are one form of witness intimidation, but intimidation can take many other forms, including:

- harassing phone calls
- communicating through third parties to the victim or the victim's family
- making annoying or repetitive contact with the victim or the victim's family
- initiating conversations that are meant to be coercive
- behaving in a way that amounts to blackmail
- stalking
- bribery

Any of this behavior could result in additional charges for the perpetrator, leading to punishment beyond what is given for the original sexual assault case. To discourage witness intimidation, prosecutors should file criminal protective orders (restraining orders) when they file the criminal charges. That way, the perpetrator will be aware of which forms of behavior are unacceptable and illegal. A victim who feels intimidated or threatened should immediately call the police, whether or not there is a protective order. A defendant can be arrested if he has violated a protective order or if there is no protective order but there are serious threats.

It is very natural for victims and victims' family members to be concerned about retaliation and threats from perpetrators. Yes, there are numerous calls and requests to dismiss charges and to be uncooperative in the prosecution of an offense. But potential physical violence has occurred in my child sexual assault cases only once. In my opinion, this is because child molesters are generally cowards who pick on kids as a method of control. Sexual assault cases are different from cases where threats and violence are the method of choice by the criminals involved.

Besides receiving the protection of orders issued by the criminal courts, victims and witnesses can go to their local civil courts and apply for restraining orders. These are particularly helpful in situations where there may not be enough to file a criminal charge, but the victim and her family want to be sure that the perpetrator cannot come into contact with the victim. Similarly, when there is a family court case where parental rights are at issue, family court judges may write an order requiring that a parent perpetrator not have contact with a child or children.

Nobody is completely safe from threats, coercion, or intimidation. Any of these should be communicated to the police immediately so they can create a safety plan for the victim.

PART SIX

HEALING AND MOVING ON

QUESTION 93: WHAT KIND OF FINANCIAL RESOURCES ARE AVAILABLE FOR THE VICTIM?

Victims of sexual assaults can receive compensation for their injuries. The victim's family may also receive compensation for financial losses that result from the victim's injury or death. Compensation can come from either the state or the offender. Most state programs cover some of the cost of medical bills, mental health treatments, lost income, and childcare services. Some states may cover relocation costs, including rent and deposits, if these are related to the victim's well-being or safety. In most states, when the offender has been convicted of the crime, the judge issues restitution for his victims, ordering him to pay for all the expenses caused by his act against the victim.

A victim or her family can apply for compensation by going to the state's government Web site or by notifying a victim's advocate to help submit their application. To receive compensation, most states require that the victim report the crime to a law enforcement or child-protective agency. To prevent fraud, a person cannot apply for compensation without first formally reporting it to a government agency.

Generally, payments are handed out based on need. If financial hardship will result if payment is not received, immediate payments to the victim or her family will be expedited. Substantial hardship occurs when a person is unable to pay for necessities, such as rent or food, once all the expenses are paid involving crime-related costs.

For practical purposes, a victim and her family should keep all insurance records, medical bills, and receipts related to the victim's injury. That way, if any issues arise regarding compensation, there will be a record of what has been spent. However, many states have laws that do not allow a victim or her family to receive compensation that is already covered by their insurance. In other words, a person may not receive additional money that goes beyond what her insurance has already covered for a particular injury. As a public policy, victim compensation programs were intended to ensure victims and their families that they can recover costs that their insurance does not cover. To protect the identity of a victim or the victim's family, confidentiality is essential. The victim's identity is disclosed only with the written permission of her guardian or family.

QUESTION 94: CAN MOLESTERS BE CURED?

Most studies conclude that molesters cannot be cured. Pedophiles in particular are increasingly regarded by psychologists as being incurable. They have been recognized as having an exclusive sexual urge to be with a prepubescent child, usually twelve years old or younger.

A parent's biggest concern is whether releasing a previously convicted molester makes that person more likely to molest again. The only evidence parents have is the molester's criminal record. However, therapists say that pedophiles and molesters do want to change but cannot. Like alcoholism and drug addiction, therapists claim that it is a disease that can be helped only through effective treatment. But finding the most effective treatment is the $64,000 question. Even if a specific treatment is effective, much like alcoholism or a smoking addiction, what guarantees do parents have that a person will not relapse, even if desperately wishing not to do so? Doubters also argue that other addictions affect only the individual involved, but with molestation, the person being harmed is an innocent child.

Because the mental health community sees pedophilia as a mental disorder, most psychologists believe that the disease can only be treated and not cured. Many types of treatments have been tried in the past with different results. For instance, in the Netherlands, pedophiles were castrated; even with this treatment, pedophiles didn't change their sexual attitude toward children. Other methods include providing offenders with medications, such as anti-testosterone pills, to help erase the sexual urges of a pedophile. Similarly, molesters are often seen as incurable because the source of their motivation to commit sexual acts comes from their minds. Many prosecutors believe that the most effective form of treatment is incarceration—the only guarantee that a molester will not molest again.

Studies have found that some people who have molested children have themselves been victims of molestation; these same studies show that many molesters have no history of sexual abuse during their childhood.

So far, there is not enough evidence to conclude whether molesters can be cured. We do know, however, that molesters can be prevented from engaging in such acts when they are incarcerated or registered as sex offenders. Be sure that, as a parent, you do whatever is necessary to ensure that your child is not exposed to a molester.

QUESTION 95: HOW SHOULD I TALK TO MY CHILD ABOUT THE ABUSE?

Speaking to your child about an abuse he or she has suffered may be traumatizing, but parents must remain calm. The most effective way to help children discuss their experiences is to show that you care. Therefore, find a quiet place familiar to the child so you are comfortable sharing information that your child may find embarrassing. Your goal should always be to make the child feel safe. Reacting strongly to a child's story can cause the child to feel shame or blame; it can also cause the child to stop sharing information about the abuse.

As a parent, trying to remain calm while extracting information about the abuse can be very tough, but these practical tips may help:

- *Make sure that the child knows it is not her fault.* Children are often sensitive and cannot process the significance of what has happened to them. Therefore, you must not allow your children to feel guilty for the terrible experiences they have suffered. Making a child feel guilty will only discourage him or her from disclosing the truth and can break any trust built up. Also, the child's abuser may have led her to believe that what was done between them was consensual or her fault. You need to be encouraging and remind your child that she had no role in the things that happened to her.

- *Be patient.* Allow your child to speak at her own pace and learn how to use the child's vocabulary. Never force your child to answer questions, you may get inaccurate or sensationalized versions of the truth, which may compromise the prosecution's criminal case against the offender.
- *Never force your children to show their injuries.* Do not make your child feel even more uncomfortable than she already is by requesting that you see her injuries. Only let your child show you her injuries with her permission. If she refuses, you should respect her decision.
- *Ask appropriate questions that do not lead to an obvious answer.* For example, do not ask, "Did Uncle Bob hurt you?" Instead, ask, "Who hurt you?" When you pose questions that do not imply that a specific person was involved, you allow the child to more accurately specify the identity of the offender and under what circumstances the acts occurred. When asking questions, use your child's vocabulary so she can understand more clearly what you are asking or saying.
- *Be honest.* Do not lie to your children. Sometimes, children do not feel that what has happened to them was illegal or even wrong. The child may still be emotionally tied to the offender and is resisting seeing him punished. Inform your child that the act was wrong and that you intend to press charges. While this may create anger and resentment, let your child know that your support for him or her comes first.

QUESTION 96: WHAT IS THE USUAL HEALING PROCESS FOR A VICTIM OF ABUSE?

First of all, everybody functions and heals differently. Anyone working with or related to a survivor of sexual assault should not have any preconceived notions about how the victim will act or feel. The keys are to be aware of the possibilities, know what phases and responses are possible, and remain supportive throughout the healing process, as long as it takes. But before healing can be completed, the survivor must give up feeling responsible and accept that it was the perpetrator who should be held accountable.

While I outline some of the stages (which collectively are commonly referred to as *rape trauma syndrome*, or RTS), know that a victim may or may not experience each stage or in the order I am listing them. Victims' reactions post-abuse are a specific type of post traumatic stress disorder. Phases may last weeks or years. Recovering from the experience of an assault may involve moving back and forth within these phases over the course of a lifetime.

The Acute Phase

In most people, the initial (acute) phase of RTS occurs right after an assault happens. Although it varies, this phase typically lasts for several weeks after the attack. People may assume that the normal response to an attack is to cry. This may be true for some survivors, but not all. A typical aspect of the acute phase may be denial and repression. The victim may exhibit either *expressed* or *controlled* emotions during this phase. Expressed responses release emotions, such as crying, laughing, shouting, and talking, among others. Controlled responses hold back the emotions. People with controlled response may seem withdrawn, resistant to talking, silent, distracted, numb, or disconnected from their feelings.

During the acute phase, a sexual assault victim may also experience noticeable changes in sleeping and eating habits. (These signs may serve to alert parents or caregivers of the assault to begin with.) Just as experiencing an assault often involves feelings of losing control over one's body, abnormal sleeping or eating habits may also raise issues of control over one's physical well-being.

Victims may be extremely aware of their physical surroundings—for example, they may be startled by unexpected sounds or occurrences. This is a typical reaction to any life-threatening or scary situation.

The Reorganization Phase

The second stage of RTS involves the survivor's attempts to reorganize his or her life after the assault's disruption. During this phase, some of the initial shock is likely to wear off, and the survivor begins to understand what happened. This phase may go on for months or even years.

Dealing with the reality of what occurred can be very painful. Survivors sometimes feel guilty or ashamed (even though being assaulted is never the survivor's fault). Despite their lack of blame, survivors may begin to hate their bodies and may use unhealthy eating patterns or other behavior to punish themselves.

Emotions commonly experienced as part of the post-traumatic stress of being assaulted include:

- shame
- fear
- guilt
- hopelessness/worthlessness
- grief
- anger
- powerlessness
- depression

Survivors may do things that seem out of character—like withdrawing from the activities and people that they usually enjoy. Sometimes, survivors may start taking part in uncharacteristically self-destructive or risky behaviors (like abusing drugs or cutting themselves) as a way to block their feelings. The effort to reorganize their lives may affect survivors' sexual relationships. For adult survivors, being sexually intimate after an assault can be scary, and they may find it difficult to be close to someone sexually. In children, this inability means that they cannot be close to adults in any appropriate way. But for others, the response is exactly the opposite. Being assaulted may cause people to feel disconnected from their bodies, and they may seek out as many sexual experiences as possible to try to erase or replace the memory of what happened.

The Resolution Phase

This is when survivors come to terms with their experiences. The survivor may still be sad, angry, or hurt, but in this phase, survivors begin to focus energy on recovering and moving forward with their lives. This does not mean that the assault is not a big deal anymore or that survivors have gotten over it—what it does mean is that they are getting stronger and learning ways to manage feelings about the assault, to feel a greater sense of control over their lives. Survivors who have reached the resolution phase can still experience flashbacks and nightmares about the assault. Flashbacks can be triggered by certain sounds, places, or smells that remind them of the assault.

QUESTION 97: WHOSE FAULT IS IT THAT MY CHILD WAS MOLESTED?

It is important for parents to know that it is not their fault if their child was molested. Parents of sexually assaulted victims often blame themselves. They focus their guilt on their inability to recognize signs that sexual abuse was occurring.

Occasionally, the mother may need to solve past issues relating to sexual abuse that she suffered, either as a child or an adult. In these situations, the sexually abused parent should seek professional help to understand and resolve issues she may have suffered but never addressed.

Parents need to remember that the act against their child was done without their permission. It was the molester's choice, not theirs, that resulted in the child's abuse. Although this does not make it easier for parents to overcome their own guilt, knowing that somebody else chose to harm their child may help them understand how little a role they had in contributing to their child's harm.

Sometimes, the blame may be on the very people we thought we trusted: our teachers, our doctors, and our pastors. These people not only may harm your child but also have a duty to report any signs of abuse or neglect that a child may be suffering. (See question 42.) Those who do not report questionable behavior may be at least partly responsible for your child's abuse; if so, you may bring a civil lawsuit or criminal charges against them.

In some cases, the parent is clearly at fault when he is a willing participant in either performing the sexual act or enabling the offender to continue the abuse by hiding it from authorities and medical professionals. Parents have a duty to protect their children once disclosure of an illegal act has occurred and they are obligated to tell local law enforcement of these acts, even if the offender is a husband or a boyfriend. Although this is not a parenting book, some simple truths about children are clear: a child's health and safety should always take precedence over the protection of another person, especially one who has committed an illegal act. A parent should always disclose the sexual acts committed against a child because of their future emotional and psychological impact. Parents must remember that children do not have the strength to say no and oftentimes are unable to recognize what is proper and what is improper behavior.

Children represent what is innocent and pure in this world. When a molester takes away a child's innocence, he is taking away everything a child believed was good. By allowing such perverse acts to continue, the parent may lead a child to believe that such behavior is "normal," an idea that will affect the child throughout his life, making him more likely to commit similar acts against other children or adults.

QUESTION 98: CAN MY CHILD VICTIM TURN INTO AN ADULT PERPETRATOR?

Many people believe that children who are victims of child sexual abuse are more likely to commit similar abuse against other children when they become adults. According to the US Department of Justice (DOJ), children who are abused or neglected are just as likely as children who are sexually assaulted to engage in future criminal sexual behavior.

However, prostitution is more prevalent in those who have been sexually assaulted as children. Sexual abuse is a traumatic experience, and some victims never deal with this trauma. These victims often struggle with depression, low self-esteem, and the constant need for attention, all of which can lead them into promiscuous lifestyles.

There are also a higher number of runaways among children who have been sexually abused. Child neglect seems to be a better indicator of future criminal behavior than child abuse. When a parent has neglected a child, the child is often lonely and cannot understand what is right or wrong. The same DOJ study points out that neglect coupled with being sexually abused does increase the likelihood that a child will commit a sex crime in the future.

On the other hand, when a child is surrounded by love and counseled after being abused, she is less likely to become a criminal. Therefore, helping the child regain shaky self-esteem is an important part of the healing process.

My conclusion is that the best antidote for a child victim who has been sexually assaulted is good parenting and counseling. Parents need to communicate to the child that he or she is always wanted and loved. To show love, parents should hug their children constantly and give words of encouragement whenever they accomplish something good—no matter how small it may be. Parents should let their children know that they can talk about anything—important or not—with them at any time. They should also do fun activities with their children, such as taking vacations, watching movies, or going to an amusement park.

Good parenting needs to be supplemented with good counseling. Counseling allows children to share information with an adult who has no previous history with them. This lets the child talk about emotions and topics that might be uncomfortable if discussed with parents. These steps can give children another means to regain their self-esteem and continue their lives as normally as possible.

QUESTION 99: CAN I TELL MY ABUSED DAUGHTER THAT SHE IS STILL A VIRGIN?

In the strictest terms, the word *virgin* is defined as a person who has not had sexual intercourse. And sexual intercourse, in its strictest terms, is the sexual union between a penis and vagina that leads to penetration. Under these terms, sexual intercourse can occur only between heterosexuals.

If I were rewriting dictionaries, I would incorporate the reality of our society in defining our terms. Virginity is not just a technical, physical term, but one that has emotional and psychological significance. When most people think of losing virginity, they are talking about the conscious decision to have consensual sexual intercourse with another person. I propose that all people use this definition of virginity: an act where a person shares his or her body with another person in the form of sexuality. It does not necessarily require a vagina, a penis, or even penetration. It is an act that is consensual—a conscious, thought-out decision. Virginity is not something that people "lose" or have "taken" but something shared with another person, like a once-in-a-lifetime sunset. If you haven't given it to a special person, it doesn't really count as being gone.

I think that people who are raped or molested are still virgins in the emotional sense, even if their bodies have had sex. They have not stopped being a virgin, nor have they experienced the emotions that go along with *giving* one's body to another. If sex is taken, not given, although one may have physically experienced it, I think it is unfair to say one is no longer a virgin. The child may still feel as if he or she is innocent and view normal sex with naivete.

Being victimized should not force you to live with a label you neither wanted nor asked for. Virginity is not something we passively lose; nonvirginity is something we deliberately choose to take. With this in mind, parents, prosecutors, medical personnel, police officers, and therapists should feel comfortable doing what Dr. Elliott Schulman does at the Rape Treatment Center at Santa Monica–UCLA Medical Center. He gives children Certificates of Virginity, regardless of what abuse they have withstood.

QUESTION 100: HOW LONG DOES THE
HEALING PROCESS TAKE?

I wish there was a simple answer to this question. Just as each person's abuse is unique, so is the healing process. I propose that certain factors may influence the healing process, either speeding it up or slowing it down.

In many ways, sexual assault is like any other traumatic event. An individual's own life experiences, family upbringing, and cultural norms will affect the process. Just as a person may seem to be on a healing path, sexual assault recovery can take a cyclical form, where it may appear that for every step forward, the victim may take one or two steps back.

The factors that influence an individual's healing process include:

- Age of the child when the abuse happened. Younger is usually more harmful, but different effects are associated with different developmental periods.
- Who committed the abuse. Effects are generally worse if it was a parent, step-parent, or trusted adult than if it was a stranger.
- Whether the child told anyone, and if so, the person's response. Doubting, ignoring, blaming, and shaming responses can be extremely harmful—in some cases even more harmful than the abuse itself.
- Whether or not violence was involved, and if so, how severe.
- How long the abuse went on.
- Whether a case was prosecuted and the victim's role in the prosecution.
- Whether the perpetrator apologized or acknowledged the abuse.

Victims may spend years trying to recover from the effects of sexual assault. Like many other traumatic events, it's often a "forgive but not forget" process in which victims may begin to forgive themselves after learning to trust other people, try to regain a sense of control over their lives, and dispell feelings of shame and guilt.

"It will always be part of the fabric of your life, but I tell people, 'You're a survivor versus a victim,'" said Ann Hagen Webb, a psychologist who has worked with abuse patients and was herself a survivor of priest abuse. Recovery from childhood sexual abuse can be a long, complicated, and often troubling process, but with proper support and therapy, full healing is possible.

APPENDIX

Where Can I Go for More Information?

There are many resources for sexual assault victims, parents and other family of sexual assault victims, and those who simply want more information.

GOVERNMENTAL AGENCIES AND PROSECUTORS' OFFICES

All states, and many counties, have their own online resources as well as hotline numbers to call for information. The Department of Justice's Web site (www.usdoj.gov) contains excellent information on the law, resources, and links to states' Web sites.

Most prosecutors' offices have a victim/witness program or a victim advocacy office that can provide detailed information on the specific legal procedures for your county or state. To find the prosecutor's office in your county, you should be able to access it from your state or county Web site. A national list of district attorney offices is available online at the National District Attorney Association (www.ndaa.org).

CRIME STATISTICS AND LEGISLATION

Bureau of Justice Assistance: www.ojp.usdoj.gov/BJA
United States House of Representatives: www.house.gov
The Constitution of the United States of America: www.law.cornell.edu/constitution
Federal Bureau of Investigation: www.FBI.gov

INTERNET SAFETY AND RESOURCES

Wired Kids, Inc.: www.wiredkids.org
National Center for Missing and Exploited Children: www.cybertipline.com
GetNetWise: www.getnetwise.com
SafeKids.com: www.safekids.com

SEXUAL ASSAULT NURSE EXAMINERS (SANE) OR SEXUAL ASSAULT RAPE TEAMS (SART) TEAMS

SANE and SART (www.sane-sart.com) are the common acronyms given for the multidisciplinary teams in each city, county, or state. Local teams can be based in a hospital, a clinic, a forensic interviewing center, or even a law enforcement office or a prosecutor's office. Any member of a multidisciplinary team can direct you to the right person to give you more information.

A MUST HAVE REGISTRY

Evidence shows that on average a child goes missing every forty seconds. Therefore, caring and responsible parents should register their child(ren) with the Amber Alert Registry in order to assist law enforcement in the most critical times.

www.amberalertregistry.org

NONPROFIT ORGANIZATIONS

Some wonderful organizations throughout the country not only provide educational information in sexual abuse prevention but also have a contact list showing to whom or where one can go to learn more or get help. Some of my favorite organizations are the following.

The Awareness Center

The Awareness Center (theawarenesscenter.org) is an international organization that addresses the issues and ramifications of sexual victimization for both adults and children in Jewish Communities.

Childhelp USA National Child Abuse Hotline

Childhelp USA is a nonprofit organization "dedicated to meeting the physical, emotional, educational, and spiritual needs of abused and neglected children." Its programs and services include this hotline, which children can call with complete anonymity and confidentiality.

> 1-800-4-A-CHILD
> (1-800-422-4453)
> TDD: 1-800-2-A-CHILD

ChildLine (UK)

According to its Web site, "ChildLine is the free helpline for children and young people in the UK. Children and young people can call us on 0800 1111 to talk about any problem—our counsellors are always here to help you sort it out."

The Innocent Justice Foundation

The Innocent Justice Foundation (innocentjustice.org) is dedicated to helping rescue children from sexual abuse. The foundation strives to significantly impact and reduce child sexual abuse in the United States through education on Internet crimes against children, victim legislative advocacy, and essential material support to law enforcement and governmental agencies that prevent, investigate, prosecute, and criminally adjudicate sex crimes against children.

> The Innocent Justice Foundation
> 132 N. El Camino Real #483
> Encinitas, CA 92024
> 760-585-8873

888-698-8873
E-mail: info@innocentjustice.org

i-SAFE

Founded in 1998, i-SAFE Inc. (www.i-safe.org) is the leader in Internet safety education. Available in all fifty states, i-SAFE is a nonprofit foundation whose mission is to educate and empower youth to make their Internet experiences safe and responsible. The goal is to educate students on how to avoid dangerous, inappropriate, or unlawful online behavior.

National Children's Alliance

Call the Children's Advocacy Center nearest you for a referral to a nearby support group or therapist specializing in child sexual abuse.

1612 K Street, NW, Suite 500
Washington, DC 20006
(800) 239-9950
(202) 452-6001
E-mail: info@nca-online.org

National Domestic Violence/Abuse Hotline

This is a twenty-four-hours-a-day hotline, staffed by trained volunteers who are ready to connect people with emergency help in their own communities, including emergency services and shelters. The staff can also provide information and referrals for a variety of nonemergency services, including counseling for adults and children and assistance in reporting abuse. They have an extensive database of domestic violence treatment providers in all fifty states and US territories. Many staff members speak languages besides English, and they have twenty-four-hour access to translators for approximately 150 languages. For the hearing impaired, there is a TDD number.

This is a good resource for people who are experiencing or have experienced domestic violence or abuse or who suspect that someone they know is being abused. *All calls to the hotline are confidential, and callers may remain anonymous if they wish.*

1-800-799-SAFE
1-800-799-7233
1-800-787-3224 TDD

National Center for Missing & Exploited Children (NCMEC)

The National Center for Missing & Exploited Children's (www.themissing.org or www.missingkids.com) mission is to help prevent child abduction and sexual exploitation, help find missing children, and assist victims of child abduction and sexual exploitation, their families, and the professionals who serve them.

National Center for Missing & Exploited Children
Charles B. Wang International Children's Building
699 Prince Street
Alexandria, VA 22314-3175
Phone: 703-274-3900
Fax: 703-274-2200
Hotline:1-800-THE-LOST (1-800-843-5678)

Rape, Abuse, Incest National Network (RAINN)

RAINN (www.rainn.org, 1-800-656-4673) has an automated service that links callers to the nearest rape crisis center. Rape crisis centers are staffed by trained volunteers and paid staff members who also understand sexual abuse issues and services (though sometimes they are not adequately prepared to refer male callers). *All calls are confidential, and callers may remain anonymous if they wish.*

BLOGS AND CURRENT LEGAL ARTICLES AND INFORMATION

RobinSax.com: www.robinsax.com
Justice Interrupted: www.justiceinterrupted.com
Women in Crime Ink: www.womenincrimeink.blogspot.com